# THE IMPACT OF INFLUENCE VOLUME 6

Using Your Influence To Create A Life Of Impact

By
**Chip Baker**

Co-authored by Powerful Influencers

2023

# THE IMPACT OF INFLUENCE

USING YOUR INFLUENCE

TO CREATE A LIFE OF IMPACT

### VOLUME 6

WRITTEN BY

## CHIP BAKER

CO-AUTHORED BY POWERFUL INFLUENCERS

Copyright © 2023 by Chip Baker

All rights reserved. This book or any portion thereof may not be reproduced or used in any manner whatsoever without the express written permission of the publisher except for the use of brief quotations in a book review or scholarly journal.

First Printing: 2023

ISBN: 978-1-7379501-9-6

Ordering Information:

Special discounts are available on quantity purchases by corporations, associations, educators, and others. For details, contact the publisher at the email listed below.

U.S. trade bookstores and wholesalers:
Please contact chipbakertsc@gmail.com.

# DEDICATION

This book is dedicated to all the people who have impacted our lives. We send a special dedication to our families and everyone who supports us. We hope that this book will leave an everlasting impact and influence many generations to come.

We are grateful for you!

# PREFACE

Dear reader,

We hope that this book will be a blessing to you. In the following chapters, you will find the lessons that these powerful authors have learned throughout their journey to success. Our hope is that you will learn from these lessons and use them to help you operate more efficiently and effectively in your life.

## Brief Description of Book

The Impact of Influence Vol. 6, Using Your Influence to Create a Life of Impact is overflowing with wisdom from visionary author, Chip Baker, and other powerful influencers who have discovered their paths to success. They are influencing many and impacting generations. The inspirational stories within the pages of this book will inspire you to make a positive difference for those around you.

# TABLE OF CONTENTS

| | |
|---|---|
| DEDICATION | vi |
| PREFACE | vii |
| LIST OF AUTHORS IN CHAPTER ORDER | 1 |
| VALUES INFLUENCE AND IMPACT | 2 |
| CREATING CHARACTER BY EXAMPLE | 8 |
| AN UNEXPECTED INFLUENCER | 16 |
| LIVE. LEARN. LEAD. | 24 |
| P A ! N | 34 |
| RT MORGAN | 42 |
| THE CHISEL IN MY JOURNEY | 50 |
| MY 2 ROLE MODELS | 60 |
| BARRIERS LEADING TO SUCCESS | 66 |
| **YOUR CIRCLE** | 74 |
| WHO IS LEADING YOU, AND, WHO ARE YOU LEADING? | 82 |
| MY WHY | 90 |
| HANGOVER | 98 |
| FREE TO FAIL: THE TENETS OF FINDING SUCCESS THROUGH FAILURES. | 106 |
| THE BUTTERFLY EFFECT | 116 |
| ABOUT THE LEAD AUTHOR | 126 |
| PICK UP THESE OTHER TITLES BY CHIP BAKER | 128 |

# LIST OF AUTHORS IN CHAPTER ORDER

1. Chip Baker
2. Brian Brogen
3. Charles Woods
4. Chaz Jackson
5. Darius Bradley, Sr.
6. Derrick Pearson
7. Dr. Jeannie Meza-Chavez
8. Kenneth Wilson
9. Leslie Davis
10. Dr. Lindsie O'Neill Almquist
11. LS Kirkpatrick
12. Manny Trujillo
13. Megan Marie Randall
14. Olaolu Ogunyemi
15. Victor Pisano

# VALUES INFLUENCE AND IMPACT
*Chip Baker*

*"Values bring value."*
*Chip Baker*

Values are the vehicle that transports our influence. This impactful vehicle can travel in many ways and be shared all over the world. Influential people are loaded with values. Values are those traits that make a difference in our world. People that have values add so much value and quality to the people around them. I have been blessed to learn from amazing people with great values.

I would like to share with you the values that those influential people had that made a positive impact on my life. Those values have provided value and substance in my life.

### Versatile

Versatile is defined as being able to do multiple things. Those people that influenced me were versatile. They were leaders and teachers, and they also volunteered their time to give service outside of the school setting. They were able to do many things. It rubbed off on others and allowed them to do many things. It influenced my life because it showed me that the more I learn, the more marketable it made me. It also allowed me to be the best version of myself so that I could give the best version of myself for others.

## Accepting

*"There is value in our differences."*
*Chip Baker*

Influential people are accepting of others. They understand that to make an impact they need to be accepting of others. They are also accepting of other ideas to have personal and professional growth. Their influence allowed me to be more accepting of others and be open to learn new things.

Growing up I was taught to be accepting of others and that everyone has value. I strive to live this out by the way I treat others. In college, I became friends with a guy. He looked nothing like me. We did not wear the same type of clothes. In fact, we did not even listen to the same type of music. Despite our differences, it did not stop me from being cordial and speaking to him when I saw him. Once we got to know each other we realized that we had similar upbringings and values. He became one of my good friends and would look out for me based off of his God given talents. He worked at a gas station in our college town. This may be showing my age but at the time there were still a few full-service gas stations in Texas. My college town was about a ten-hour drive from my hometown. I had an older car and before going home for breaks he would tell me to bring the car by so he could check it out. Sometimes he would change the oil and make other suggestions on things I needed. He would do this for me to make sure I had a safe trip. He continued to do this throughout my years in college. What if I was not taught to be accepting? Being accepting gave me the opportunity to meet and learn from people that are different than me. It has benefitted me tremendously. I am grateful for that, and I continue to promote the idea of being accepting of others. There is value in our differences.

## Loving

*"Love is a trait that influences and adds value."*
*Chip Baker*

Love is the glue that binds our world together. The people in my life that influenced me always showed love. When I was in college my friends would get a chance to be around my parents and grandparents. My friends would get these opportunities when my family would come to football games or when they would visit my hometown. My friends would be so blown away by the fact that my family would hug them and be open to learn about them and their families. It showed me that showing love to others is so important. My friends still tell me stories about meeting certain family members and the great conversations they had. Love is a trait that influences and adds value. That love has been given back to me from so many people because my family has shown love to them. Love conquers all.

## Understanding

Understanding is being aware and comprehending what is going on in various situations. It involves filling the social emotional tank of others. In a vehicle, if the gas tank is empty the vehicle is not able to move. In life, a person's social emotional tank must have fuel to live a fulfilled and influential life. When people exhibit understanding they fill the social emotional tank of others. This causes a dynamic ripple effect of people understanding others, which changes generations in a positive way.

## Enthusiastic

*"Enthusiasm is infectious and contagious."*

In high school I was blessed to have a coach in my life that was enthusiastic in how he approached his day-to-day tasks. His actions showed us that it was ok to enjoy our career. I was always excited to go to his class and also see what he was going to teach when coaching us. You could tell that he wanted to be there and that he loved what he did. He was living out his calling. The experience is one of the experiences that influenced me to become a teacher/coach. Once I became a teacher-coach I strived to operate in the same manner. I strived to be enthusiastic because I knew, by experience, that it would be infectious and contagious.

## Sentimental

When I hear the word sentimental, I think of someone being intentional about showing love and genuine concern. When I hear the word sentimental, I also think of effort! Effort, love, and genuine concern shows that a person cares about you. Those influential people showed that they are sentimental by exhibiting those traits.

They did not have to go above and beyond to try. They did not have to go above and beyond to show me love. They did not have to go above and beyond to have genuine concern for me. They did, and it has influenced my life. It influenced my life in such a manner that it has impacted me and caused me to be the person I am today.

Values are the means of transportation that influences and impacts people for generations. There have been amazing people that have influenced me in my life by exhibiting some great values. Those traits were versatile, accepting, loving, understanding, enthusiastic and sentimental. God bless you on your journey to influence and impact! Go get it!

# VALUES

*V- Versatile*
*A-Accepting*
*L- Loving*
*U- Understanding*
*E- Enthusiastic*
*S- Sentimental*

**ABOUT THE AUTHOR:**

See Lead Author's Bio in About the Author section.

## CREATING CHARACTER BY EXAMPLE
**Brian Brogen**

I have had numerous influences in my life, too many to list and acknowledge in this chapter. I will share a few that are noteworthy and have impacted my life and how I live it today.

My parents divorced when I was fourteen years old. I did not enjoy their tumultuous relationship and often felt like it wouldn't or couldn't last. I was devastated and bitter when they eventually divorced. I expressed my feelings through fits of rage and anger, punching holes through doors and kicking holes in walls.

I was on the cusp of becoming a juvenile delinquent committing minor crimes of shoplifting, underage drinking, vandalism, truancy, and more. On one occasion skipping school and stealing cigarettes, I was delivered to school from the back of a police car at class change. Many of my classmates got the entertainment of seeing me pulled from a police car and delivered to the principal's office. That was humiliating.

These behaviors and my desire to not live with either parent landed me in a youth home. After being in this home for several weeks and learning about the difficult lives of the other youth in the home, I decided I did not have it so bad after all.

I was raised in a middle-class neighborhood in a small-town suburban community. Many of the other youth in the home were raised in the ghetto and lacked the love and nurture I had from both of my parents. A few were car thieves and there was even one who had been associated with attempted murder. My parents may not have been able to get along with each other, however they truly loved me and my sister. I quickly realized I did not belong in this youth home and needed to go back home.

My mom had begun a relationship with a longtime friend of the family, he was on the receiving end of my rage. At the time I agreed with my dad that he had betrayed the family by dating my Mom. I let him know he was not my dad and would never take the place of my dad. I now know that was never his intention.

While in the youth home he began to show care and concern for me. He visited me with my mom. They wrote greeting cards expressing how much they missed me and wanted me to come home. I began to let my guard down and allow him to be part of my life. My Mom and Ronnie became engaged, and I had to accept him as my stepdad.

Ronnie is a mentor who became an influence in my life. He was a country boy and taught me respect for myself and others. This was much needed as an early teenager to bring some structure to my life. My Mom worked at a newspaper and advanced through the company, eventually becoming an executive. Ronnie was a minister. His schedule allowed him to become the parent who handled my mischievous ways during high school.

There were many occasions where I was the class clown or troublemaker. On one of many trips to the assistant principal's office, he shared with me his system of recommending troubled students to be transferred to the "opportunity school" commonly referred to as Opp. He showed me the index card where he kept account of my shenanigans and said, "Brian, I usually refer students to be transferred to Opp when the front of this card is full."

It was clear that my card was full on the front. He then turned it over to reveal the back half of the card filled in. As he wrote in my latest infraction. He warned me, "This is your last warning. If I see you in this office again you will be going to Opportunity School."

I will share one of these shenanigans and the lessons I learned:

My stepdad picked me up from school after wrestling practice. I had a blood-stained shirt and he wanted to know why. I began to tell him my made-up version of what happened. "I was messing around at the tennis court, and someone was chasing me. I slipped. When I went to fall, I grabbed the chain link fence and it cut the inside of my arm." I had practiced this story and was convinced I could be convincing.

## You're Caught

He then handed me the hat I had been wearing when I fell through the ceiling of the wrestling coach's office. The hat with my name inside the bill. Our neighbor and the principal of the high school had given it to him. I had neglected to pick up my hat in my haste to leave the debris of insulation, ceiling tile, and metal grid scattered in the drop zone on the floor of the coach's office.

Our coach had taught us how to enter his office through the ceiling when his keys were locked in the office. I needed to use the phone before practice. I thought I would try to enter over the wall and through the ceiling. However, on this trip, I lost my balance and crashed through the ceiling. I fell eight feet and landed on a trophy desk. Then, with cat like instincts, I jumped up, ran out of the office, and skipped practice.

## Lesson Learned

I learned a valuable lesson that day and the following weeks during Saturday school. The principal had calculated the cost of the damages and determined that I owed the school my labor in exchange for the expensive repairs.

# Be Honest

Honesty is truly the best policy. In my case, had I fessed up with my coach, he may have handled it differently without involving the principal or my stepdad.

My stepdad encouraged me to be honest and take my punishment like a man. He told me that lying creates webs that are hard to navigate. He said the truth will come out eventually, so own up to it.

During the rebellious times I lashed out and was hateful with my mom, he told me that I owed my Mom the utmost respect. I watched him give his own Mother the utmost respect. I decided that I wanted to follow his example and show my mom the love and respect she deserved. He truly treated his mother like the queen she was, and I needed to do the same.

One of the most difficult times in my life was finding out that my stepdad had taken his own life. I would never have believed this in a million years. He had just retired from pastoring for over thirty years and turned seventy years old a few months before. He left his children and grandchildren devastated, creating a huge void in their lives.

I am grateful that I expressed my feelings of gratitude to him for his influence in my life a few months before. This experience has given me a whole new appreciation for the importance of mental health. I wish I could have encouraged him to keep living for his family. I encourage you to recognize those who have had an impact in your life before it is too late. I also encourage you to look for signs of mental illness and intervene as much as you can. Suicide happens too often in this world, and we need to work diligently to prevent it.

I will now share another positive influence in my life and the lessons learned from him.

I entered the construction industry immediately after working one summer as a stockman in a grocery store. My first role as a seventeen-year-old was as a shipping clerk and "gopher." Because of insurance restrictions, they did not permit me to operate or be around heavy equipment. However, I had a driver's license and was ready to "go for" this and "go for that." They sent me to get a much-needed tool or materials required to complete a project.

When I turned eighteen, I was eager. I was finally allowed to work with the other adults around the noisy and powerful construction equipment. I wanted to show my capability to produce alongside some weathered and hardened construction craftsmen.

One of my first opportunities to "pull my weight" and "earn my stripes" was on a crew assembling industrial conveyors. We were attaching large rolling idlers to big steel frames with huge bolts and massive wrenches. It was fascinating and rewarding to see parts and pieces assembled into working machinery.

I was full of zeal and vigor to be a productive team member and graduate from gopher to craftsman. We needed a tool to continue our assembly work and remain productive on one occasion. As a former gopher, I knew which supply house had the tool we needed, and I was familiar with procuring this tool.

I jumped into making it happen. I signed out the company truck, drove to the supply house, picked up the tool we needed, and raced back to keep the crew productive. I was expecting a hero's welcome. When I returned an hour later with the problem solved, much to my chagrin, a perturbed supervisor who wanted to know my whereabouts met me. He told me the big boss wanted to see me. Uh oh! What have I done?

I headed to the office. On the way, I had a knot in my stomach like I used to have on my frequent visits to the principal's office during my troubled school years.

I sheepishly entered the office. The big boss had questions about where I had been and why I had left the site without the supervisor's permission. I explained why I had taken these actions. While he understood my motives, he informed me of company policies and procedures. He explained how the supervisor is responsible for the crew and their needs. He has to know where they are and what they are doing.

He instructed me to get permission before leaving the worksite in the future.

Then he encouraged me with these words, "Brian, you are an aggressive person by nature, but you must harness that aggression and use it purposefully and thoughtfully."

I have now encouraged countless other individuals with this simple message, "Harness your aggression."

Over the years, I have learned that unharnessed aggression leads to destroyed relationships in careers, friendships, and family.

Thankfully, the big boss was a wise leader. He knew how to deliver a correction message, soften the blow by recognizing potential, and not smothering my desire to be a productive team member. This mentor has been a confidant and staunch supporter of mine for a few decades now.

A great mentor knows how to hold others accountable, recognizes their potential, sees their strengths, and encourages them to be the best version of themselves. I have had many mentors. I would not be where I am today without their guidance and encouragement.

As Stan Toler says in the book Minute motivators for leaders, "Every leader should be a mentor, but every leader should have a mentor."

## Values of a Mentor:

They are patient – mentors understand that their mentees need time to develop. You can't train experience; you gain experience through action, trial, and error.

They communicate well – mentors are excellent listeners and seek to understand the needs of the mentee.

They are models of leadership – mentors set the example. They aren't perfect, but they are conscience that others are following them and mirroring their actions.

They come to where you are – mentors have an ability to recognize where another person is, get on their level to communicate with them, and bring them along to the desired outcome.

They recognize potential – mentors see the potential in an individual. They recognize their strengths and guide that individual to their fullest potential.

In conclusion, I challenge you as a leader and a mentor to look around, see others who you can add value to as their mentor, reach your hand out to them, and challenge them. Find a mentor, reach your hand out to them, and be challenged by them. We can create a chain of mentorship and make the world a better place. As with the parts and pieces that come together to assemble a working piece of machinery, we can come together as a community and create a better society.

## ABOUT THE AUTHOR:

Social Media:
**LI** @brianbbrogen
**Website** https://buildcs.net
**Email** brian.brogen@gmail.com

Brian Brogen is a Coach, Trainer, and Speaker with an emphasis on communication and team building. As a certified human behavior expert, Brian has a knack for developing teams and individuals both personally and professionally. Brian works with organizations and individuals, coaching and training using his experience, knowledge, tenacity, and sense of humor. Brian is the founding author of Voices For Leadership™ a collaboration of 40 diverse authors sounding their unique voice on leadership principles.

Brian is the best-selling author of The 100-Hour Pilot. Brian enjoys flying with friends and family as a hobby.

Signature Speaking and Workshop Topics

Executing Excellence with a P.L.A.N.

Hear and Be Heard

The Benefits of Mentorship

5 Keys for Successful Collaboration

## AN UNEXPECTED INFLUENCER
**Charles Woods**

"Everyday you wake up is a new opportunity, it's up to each person to choose what you do with that opportunity."
-Danny Cottonham

"There are nine billion people on this planet but only one you. Be the very best version of you that's possible!"
-Danny Cottonham

"Regardless of your background, zip code, or poverty status you can still make it in this world."
-Danny Cottonham

    You don't always have the choice of what type of influencer is put in your life. You do have the choice whether or not to allow the influence of a perceived influencer to impact your life. The realization that these types of choices are not always ingrained in our minds can be scary. We are not always privy to conversation about carefully choosing the right influencer, but these choices are a huge part of who we are and who we are to become.
    Life can surprise you by putting people in your life that will leave an everlasting impression on you and those around you. Never being a person that needed to be in large crowds, or the center of

attention, it was a unique situation when I infused myself in someone's life. I didn't really look up to many men, so it was a big deal when I put that type of energy into someone and took time to share my space.

In late July of 1995 I began a new chapter in my life. Nothing around me was familiar. No one knew who I really was or my life story. Yes, some knew my name and the city that I came from, but not the true me. Unlike many of my peers there was no fear, just excitement. The excitement for this opportunity to be in control of my life. No one could ruin this opportunity but me and the choices that I made.

Earlier that Spring, February 5, 1995, I chose to sign a five-year football scholarship to the University of Southwestern Louisiana, known today as the University of Louisiana Lafayette. When I arrived on campus, I had no idea what to expect, but there was no turning back. One special day during our freshman summer workout, the coaching staff introduced the freshmen football players to one of the most influential men that I know, Mr. Danny Cottonham. Everyone calls him Mr. C. He was our athletic academic adviser. He was the extra layer of support for all athletes that came through the university.

1. He made sure we were communicating with our academic advisors.
2. He kept us on track in our degree programs.
3. He made sure we were prepared and doing everything in our power to remain academically eligible to participate in our chosen sport.

Mr. C had the most important job in the athletic department. If we could not take care of those three items we could not participate or continue to participate in our collegiate sport. This would cause a negative trickle effect for those athletic programs.

**4 P's**

"Plan, Practice, Passion, Practice again."
-Danny Cottonham

"Passion is what makes you get up in the morning. Passion will make easy the things that most people find difficult."
-Danny Cottonham

"Don't be afraid to change, it's the path to getting better."
-Danny Cottonham

A high level of patience is essential when ensuring a successful interaction with young adults. The patience to wait and listen. The patience to guide and mentor. Patience seemed to be second nature and one of Mr. C's strongest traits. He knew how to communicate with anyone he encountered while also making you feel heard, encouraged, and supported. Mr. C took the time to pour into young adults with resources and strategies that would successfully support their transition through different stages of their lives. He gave individuals the chance to be better as they worked through the challenges of life; learning from the good and the bad, their successes and failures.

It can be discouraging when you turn on the television, log in to social media, or sit with a group of people and the majority of the focus is on negative topics. Why do the negative topics get the most attention? Why is it so hard to be positive? Mr. C on the other hand is a beacon of positivity when everyone else may be struggling. Mr. C found ways to infuse a positive mindset amongst the individuals involved, regardless of the situation. He is the person that individuals seek out when they need to be motivated or just need someone to listen. The GREAT thing about these interactions is that Mr. C is not always telling you what you want to hear. He makes it a point to tell you what you need to hear, and with his delivery you have no choice but to receive his message. A true man for the people!

Mr. C has every reason to be negative but chooses to lead with positivity. He is paralyzed from the waist down and confined to a wheelchair due to a serious accident on campus just four months after his graduation from then USL (now UL) and being hired at the young age of twenty two to serve as Assistant Dean of Student Personnel. He has had multiple surgeries to address different complications and concerns. He has been in the hospital several times for medical concerns outside of his surgeries and from previous surgeries that would send many of us over the edge. I am grateful and humbled to have Mr. C in my life as well as witness him lead with so much selflessness, grace, and humility.

"The best sign of maturity is your ability to say no."
-Danny Cottonham

"A bad circle of friends will eventually become a cage."
-Danny Cottonham

When it comes to your circle and who you allow in your circle, Mr. C is a first round pick. He is the type of individual that will empower others to do better, which will lead them to be better. Your circle is a very important part of your success. GREAT men like Mr. C are integral to the development of a thriving, supportive, successful circle. Mr. C could easily use his situation as the reason why he couldn't do this or that, instead he puts his situation to the side and focuses on being a servant leader for others. In fact, his situation never comes up unless he is asked. Mr. C has been one of my motivators for over twenty plus years and I continue to be moved by his acts of kindness and intentionality.

Mr. C served thirty years supervising in the area of academic support services for all USL/UL student athletes with a total of thirty five years in time spent as a University Administrator. He is a pillar for my Principals of GREATness. When I think about some of the individuals that live the five traits of GREAT, Mr. C is unquestionably one of those individuals.

Gratitude - Mr. C shows his gratitude for being able to impact the lives of each individual that he encounters. He does not take these relationships for granted. He pours just as much or more into these relationships as those individuals.

Resilient - Mr. C shows an enormous amount of resilience through all his trials and tribulations while continuing to push himself and others to be better.

Energy - Mr. C leads with positive energy when most would waiver. He focuses on what he can control and does not worry about those situations that he can't.

Accountability - Mr. C is accountable for his actions and how he presents himself to others. He does not need someone hovering over him to make sure he is doing what is right. Mr. C lives by what is right.

Trust - Mr. C builds trust with those in his care as well as anyone he encounters. Everyone around Mr. C knows that he has their best interest at heart. You are in GREAT hands with Mr. C.

If I could live one percent of my life as Mr. Danny Cottonham does, I would be living a GREAT life. I am truly blessed to have Mr. Danny Cottonham as a friend, mentor, and fraternity brother. We are both members of the GREATest fraternity in the world, Kappa Alpha Psi Fraternity, Inc. and he is one of the main reasons I became a member of this GREAT organization. I had a choice and allowing Mr. C in my circle was one of the best choices I could have made. He has made me a better man and I hope I have done the same for him. Be in control of your choices and don't be afraid to minimize the number of individuals you allow in your life. You want to be around people that add value to you. You should also add value to them. These types of moves are in your control!!!

"All I am and all I was able to do was only done by the Grace of God!"
-Danny Cottonham

"The difference between pride and humanity; pride cares about who's right, humanity cares about what's right."
-Danny Cottonham

"Your circle is your circle!!! You control your memberships!!!"
-Charles Woods

## ABOUT THE AUTHOR:

Social Media:
**LI** @Charles Woods
**Website** charles-woods.square.site
**Email** woodzworxgroup@gmail.com

Charles has twenty plus years in public education, nine years as a classroom teacher and football coach, six years as a head boys track coach, five years as an assistant principal and this year makes his sixth year as a building principal.

Charles has a M.S. in Engineering and Technology Management and a B.S. in Industrial Technology from the University of Louisiana at Lafayette. He is a multiple time best-selling author for his collaborative work in The Winning Mindset, Black Men Love and The Impact Of Influence Volume 1, 2, 4, and 5 as well as his work as the visionary author of Concrete Connections. Charles is a servant leader that takes pride in having a Positive Mindset and being a Mentor, Coach and Speaker.

Charles is married to his beautiful wife Celena Woods and has two daughters Courtney and Chelsea Greer.

His certifications include:

EC-12 Superintendent Certification

EC-12 Principal Certification

EC-12 Special Education Certification

Rice University Leadership Partner's Executive Education Academy

Non-Crisis Intervention Trainer

"There is no other profession that gives me the opportunity to impact lives like public education. I did not choose this path; this path chose me. I will continue to be a servant leader to those in my care and for those that choose to work with me. I am forever grateful for this opportunity to make a difference in the lives of others. I live to serve, I do not serve to live!"

"Don't be a product of your environment, make your environment a product of a positive you!!!"

## LIVE. LEARN. LEAD.
### Chaz Jackson

Along my journey, I have discovered that influence is the capacity to impact the character, growth, or actions of someone or something. When I personally think of influence, a candle comes to mind. A candle's purpose is to provide light to a dark space.

> "In the same way, let your light shine before others, that they may see your good deeds and glorify your Father in heaven."
> - Matthew 5:16

We all hold the candle of influence inside us! It doesn't matter your gender, skin color, where you were born, or the circumstances that have happened to you. Your story and experiences are designed to create change in others. We all have the gift to provide light to someone's life who could be going through adversity, challenge, opposition, or just looking for someone to bring positivity into their life.

Take a moment and think about who lit the candle of influence for you?

A teacher who helped you achieve a personal milestone or goal.
A coach who helped you become a better athlete or leader.
Someone who lifted you up during a tough time in your life.
A friend who went the extra mile for you.

How did it make you feel? Now, think about how their candle influenced success in your life! Their influence helped you live, learn, and lead toward the greatest version of yourself. Over the years, there have been some amazing candle lighters or positive influencers that have impacted my life. I am led to share three points, and after each concept, a daily challenge is mentioned to encourage action steps. Let's dive deep into it family!

## LIVE TO CREATE

Do you think of yourself as someone creative? It's easy to dismiss this part of yourself, but it's a mistake to ignore the importance of creativity. You are gifted differently to make a difference! Do you know why? Because GREATNESS made you, therefore GREATNESS is within YOU! You were born to create!

Tapping into your creativity will allow your GREATNESS to echo influence in every area of your life and to those you serve. Creativity will help you overcome adversity and bounce back from every mistake. Are you asking yourself, how will creativity help me achieve more and develop a better mindset? Your ability to create will help you see the potential in the world. It will guide you to more impact and influence in the lane God calls you to serve.

Nothing can hold you back if you can creatively come up with solutions to any problem. Albert Einstein once said, "It's not that I'm so smart, it's just that I stay with problems longer." I love this quote. From my experience, if you're able to stay with problems longer like Einstein states, and see connections others have never made before, your confidence will soar, and just about everything will be possible.

I encourage you to allow yourself time to think, create and see solutions to your problems. You'll start to see that the world is wide open to you and that nothing is standing in your way. Your mind is incredible and can take you places you never thought possible. You have the power to empower people, inspire hope and transform lives.

I take the daily challenge of allowing creativity to come to me. Part of this is giving myself time to rest and reflect. How is this area in your life? You've probably heard creative people say that their best ideas come to them in the shower or on a long walk. That's because sometimes you must turn your mind off for your GREATNESS within to get to work.

You might think it's hopeless because you don't view yourself as a naturally creative person. Maybe you're constantly jealous because other people seem to come up with better ideas than you. Don't limit yourself like that. It is not true—LIVE TO CREATE!

## TAKE THE DAILY CHALLENGE

Take time off from the daily grind. It will help if you recharge your batteries.

Examine all angles of a problem.

Look to others for inspiration.

## LEARN TO BE MORE GRATEFUL

Do I have permission to ask a tough question? How much time do you spend complaining and feeling sorry for your circumstances? We all fall into the habit of doing it way too much. Science has discovered the more you complain, will eventually lead to being ungrateful. If all you can see are the bad things, you will attract even more "bad things" into your life.

It's important to make a consistent effort to see the good in life. Things might seem hard sometimes, but it's important to stay optimistic. No matter how hard life gets, there is good in the world. There is good you can bring into your life to be happier and live more fully. One of the best ways to get started is to learn to be more grateful.

We often complain without thinking about it—whether in our own mind or out loud. It's even the most popular or expected thing to do sometimes. It's a social thing to complain about your boss or how hard your job, school, life, kids, and responsibilities are. It's like we sometimes try to one-up each other with how difficult everything is. If you notice a negative thought entering your mind, take the daily challenge to replace it with a positive idea. It's OK to be upset and disappointed about things, of course.

You should never let anything get you down so much that you can't see a way out. You shouldn't just complain just for the sake of it. Try to find the good wherever you can. A big part of this is trying to surround yourself with positive people. There are certain people out in the world who live to complain. It doesn't matter how great or easy something is. It doesn't matter how positive you are about it, these people will find something to complain about. Unfortunately, negativity can be as infectious as a yawn.

> "And be not conformed to this world: but be ye transformed by the renewing of your mind, that ye may prove what is that good, and acceptable, and perfect, will of God."
> - Romans 12:2

Right now, you're in a battle for positivity. As you read this, maybe you're tired of living the life you're living right now. That means it's time to cut off the negative, joy-sucking vampires or create healthy boundaries to protect yourself. Only hang out with those people once you're strong enough to laugh off their negativity and focus on the positive instead. Learn to be grateful for the great things in your life, no matter how bad things may seem. Slowly but surely, life will get better and more manageable. Fall in love with the process!

## TAKE THE DAILY CHALLENGE

Keep a gratitude journal if you want to consciously remain grateful every day. Journal about the wonderful things that happen to you each day. Journal about how grateful you are that you have the intelligence, drive, and creativity to solve any problem that comes your way. Write in a way that will attract even more positivity and abundance into your life.

You can journal when you wake up in the morning, before sleep at night, or both. The more you do it, the more aware you'll become of the positive things in your life. The more aware you are of positivity, the more abundantly you'll live your life. Being grateful and keeping a gratitude journal is a simple step, but it will lead to major changes in your life.

## LEAD TOWARD THE IMPOSSIBLE

Do you like to run? For two thousand years of human history, people worldwide believed the same thing. No human being can run a mile in less than four minutes.

Until one person did! He achieved the impossible. Even when he didn't have support from family and friends. They thought he had lost his mind! The Dr told him. "Your HEART will explode; please don't do it."

Has someone ever told you not to think a certain way? Doubted you? These labels have been placed on me before! And that's what Roger Bannister heard from the world when he decided to try and break the world record of running one mile in under four minutes.

On May 6th, 1954, he ran a mile in under four mins, and guess what? He didn't die. He overcame the labels, doubts, and limiting beliefs. He shattered everything we thought we knew about human limitations. He ran the mile in three minutes 59.4 seconds. Roger Bannister did it! He achieved the impossible. And how long did it take the next guy to do it? Forty-six days.

Remember, for two thousand years of human history, the world believed running a mile in under four minutes was impossible. What changed? Did the human body magically evolve overnight so it could run faster? The body stayed the same. The mindset and attitude changed.

Before Roger Bannister, no one ever tried to run a mile in under four minutes. They accepted the impossible! Bannister paved the way for others to believe that the impossible is possible.

What animal is the king of the jungle? If you guessed the lion, you are correct!

Why do you think the lion is the king of the jungle? His mindset and attitude make him king.

It is not because of his height; the giraffe is the tallest. It's not because he is the biggest or strongest. That is the elephant. The smartest is the chimpanzee, and the fastest is the cheetah. It is the lion's mindset and attitude that make him KING.

Roger Bannister was not the:
Tallest
Biggest
Strongest
Smartest
Fastest

But, like the lion, Bannister's mindset and attitude allowed him to achieve things that may seem impossible to others!

Like the four-minute mile, everything in this world was impossible until someone with a positive mindset, attitude, and self-discipline made it possible. What have you been holding back on because someone told you it wasn't possible? You have the same potential as Roger Bannister, physically, mentally, and emotionally. I want to encourage you to be the Roger Bannister in your family! And, when I say Roger Bannister, I mean regardless of the naysayers, obstacles, barriers, circumstances, or statistics you may face, you remain steadfast, go after your dreams, and strive for your goals.

You could be the first in your family to go to college and change the belief that people with your last name couldn't achieve a college degree. You can change belief at your school or workplace. You could be the first to talk with that one person you have been avoiding because of fear and what others might say. You could be the first to speak up at practice or during a game when a teammate is in the wrong. You could be the first to stand up for someone being mistreated. You could be the first to stand up for what is right. What have you been holding back on because someone told you it wasn't possible?

Martin Luther King, Jr. says, "The ultimate measure of a man is not where he stands in comfort or convenience but where he stands during challenge and controversy." For us to do something that has yet to be done, we must believe it first and be willing to have the courage to overcome the obstacles standing in our way.

Are you ready?

Lead toward the IMPOSSIBLE!

## TAKE THE DAILY CHALLENGE

To be able to choose our response is our greatest weapon. It contributes towards a sense of control and empowerment. Take the daily challenge when adversity comes knocking. Welcome it. See it as an opportunity to learn and grow. And watch a major shift take place in your life. Adversity, challenge, and opposition will always be with us. Our attitude and perspective will help us move through it.

Never stop being a student. Always try to find a lesson in everything. Our experiences are designed to teach others, not obstacles, to hold us back!

Remember to...

LIVE TO CREATE
LEARN TO BE MORE GRATEFUL
LEAD TOWARD THE IMPOSSIBLE

Thanks for diving deep into this inspirational read with me! If you enjoyed this chapter or find it helpful, I would be grateful if you post a short review on Amazon. I encourage you to follow all the authors on social media. Your support for the authors in this book, really makes a difference. You are gifted differently to make a difference. Continue to be God's Echo! Peace.

## ABOUT THE AUTHOR:

Social Media:
**LI** @chaz-jackson-5b2847155
**Website** www.chazjacksonspeaks.org
**Email** chaz@chazjacksonspeaks.org

"Chaz" Jackson is a bestselling author, certified facilitator and leadership speaker, podcast host, and licensed healthcare professional. Chaz is passionate about helping others harness the greatness inside of them and learn productive ways to unleash their unique greatness in a harmonious and loving way to the world.

You are gifted differently, to make a difference!

# P A ! N
**Darius Bradley Sr.**

4:56 AM December 13, 2022, I experienced the most intense life altering pain and beauty that I ever have all at once.

My beloved mother, Connie, transitioned from physical form to spirit energy. My younger sister, Shantel, and I held her in our arms, rubbed her head and her face. We shared words of comfort and love as our mother laid as still as a sculpted canvas. I stood on the right side and my sister on the left of our mother's medical bed, we surrounded our beautiful Mother with agape love. As she deeply inhaled, then exhaled, our mother blessed the two of us with the greatest gift that anyone could ever receive, her last breath. The pa!n is truly ineffable though accompanied by paralleling solace that our mother no longer has to suffer and fight. Her tremendously prostrating uphill climb as a grieving mother due to the loss of her first-born child, our big brother, Derrick, just a year before, along with her medical conditions, has now yielded her peace. My mother-in-law, Jemenda, transitioned six months before my mom. While I was still mourning my big bro, I had to focus my energy towards my beautiful wife, Desiree, while she grieved the loss of her beloved mother. We grew stronger together underpinning each other, as we went through the pa!n we were feeling from the passing of the two beautiful women who gave birth and so much more to each of us.

Life will not always be smiles, laughter, and good times. There will be moments of contrast. That's inevitable. I have learned that PA!N, though it may hurt, is not here to hurt us. It is an instrument of indication. It enables us to identify who we are, what we can or cannot do, who we can become, and how it will benefit us. Life experiences can alter our expectations. Disturbances are needed to disrupt the default behaviors. How do we respond when an army of Goliath's ambush our way of life? Anything can be a trigger that transforms one's essence. As my extremely beautiful wife, Desiree would say, "You can become bitter or better," when faced with the hardships in life.

It's my personal belief that nothing can prepare you for such contrasting times as experience does. I know this to be a fact all too well. Going through the emotions of loved ones transitioning started when I was only fifteen years old with my father, Irwin Byron Bradley. He was a loving, GOD'S living word, phenomenal man, husband, father and beyond.

One of my greatest pains is having a child that I wish I could do more for. My wife and I are extremely blessed with three amazing kids! Our oldest son is Darius Jr. Our daughter, Deonc, is our second. Our baby boy, Daniel, is also known as Bubba/Bub! Our daughter, Deonc, was born with over twenty-seven different diagnoses. Just recently, the medical team found and added two more diagnoses to her already extended list. Jarcho-Levin which is a skeletal deformity is the most highlighted. It is a very rare syndrome. In our daughter's case, it is so severe that it caused discrepancy in her respiratory system, leaving her unable to breathe on her own. She's also deaf, so as a family we are all learning how to communicate with sign language. Deonc lived the first seven months of her life in NICU. Now, she stays in the comfort of her own bedroom. As a family we have grown spiritually, mentally, physically, and beyond.

As a husband and father my every heartbeat is committed to my family. It pains me that my best efforts, at times, are not enough to build a better quality of life for my daughter. To see her on the ventilator every day, and all that she must do to function, commands me to always be my best. Tears flow as I witness my two sons love, care, and support their sister unconditionally. The tears of gratitude, love, sadness, and happiness flow. They trace my face as if they were a second skin. Our sons have never expressed verbally that they have reservations about the attention their sister receives. At times I wonder if they feel that we do not invest as much time in their everyday lives as we do in their sister's, who is medically dependent.

Both Darius Jr. and Daniel are very talented, intelligent and set out to GO GET !T in every area of their lives. They have trying times as we all do, but they continue to push forward knowing that as a family we always support each other. It's not easy at times, but it's worth it to give your undivided attention to those who are in your life; especially your kids and spouse, no matter what the challenges may be. Sacrifices will be made in the process. It's a must that we strategically, intentionally, and consistently make those sacrifices to enable equal time for those who matter most in our lives. My kids and wife are my heartbeats, my world, and my entirety. I've learned that it's the broken pieces that grant us the greatest opportunity to build a life of organic beauty.

We all go through seasons. In each season there's so much to learn. At times the lessons, subjects, or teachers are not the most favorable. It's the lesson that's clothing our blessing. We discover who we truly are when our atmosphere is disturbed. Our health, finances, or relationships may be compromised. Until we come to that fork in the road, our travels are at a certain level of comfort that we can manage. What happens when we are in an abyss of tangled emotions? Our hearts are racing, we're breathing frantically, and reaching out but there's nothing to grab. There's nothing to stand on and it seems as if nobody is there? Those disturbances shake us in a way that we've never been shaken and provoke us to move like we've never moved before. It enables us to develop muscle spiritually, mentally, and physically. I discovered that by going through some of my darkest days.

I remember the times that I reacted instead of responding to my situations. I felt the buildup of atomic tension rising within my entirety. At any moment, an emotional explosion could occur. It would cause irreparable damage to myself and others! For example, when my father passed away when I was fifteen, I was mad at the world! I became someone I didn't even recognize. I was ready to fight anyone, for any reason. I was speaking to my mother in a disrespectful tone. I began acting out in ways that didn't reflect the way my mother and father raised me. That behavior followed me into my adulthood because I had not learned how to respond instead of reacting.

REACTING to a situation occurs when we add the letters (AL) at the end of the word EMOTION. The word becomes emotional, which means that we voluntarily give up our control. RESPONDING to a situation by not adding the letters (AL) yields us control. It allows us to feel the emotions, go through the emotions, and grow to understand. This helps us to resolve our situations more effectively. It is easier said than done, but it's worth doing for us and especially for those who matter most in our lives. I can't say that when I discovered the practice of Responding instead of Reacting that everything became easier instantly. It didn't. In fact, things became more challenging as the resistance increased. Applying the practice of Responding enables me to position my antennas in a direction that grants me a better reception. When put in a difficult position we have two choices, React or Respond.

I was placed in that position when our princess Deonc's life was at risk! I had a situation at work that caused me to split my pants. I had to leave work to go and change my attire into something more suitable, then return to work, so I thought. The moment I arrived home I fumbled with my keys at the front door. While trying to fit the key to open the door, I heard my daughter's distress alarm going off on her ventilator. The entire time I was trying to open my door, her alarm had been sounding off. I immediately knew that something was wrong. I could feel it in my spirit!

My wife was at work. Our son Darius Jr. was at school. Daniel had not yet been born. The only people in the house at the time were my daughter and her nurse. When I finally managed to open the door and enter our home, I could hear our daughter's alarm! While running through the house to my daughter's room, I discovered the nurse comfortably sitting on the chair. She was enjoying her lunch and conversation on her cellphone. To my surprise the nurse continued talking, laughing, and eating with no response to me. I looked over to witness our daughter unresponsive, eyes rolled to the back of her head, foaming from her mouth, and drenched in sweat. Imagine a beautiful little girl weighing only about sixteen pounds, connected to a life support machine. She's deaf and medically dependent, lying lifeless right before your eyes. That beautiful little girl is your daughter!

I was in disbelief! I urgently moved towards my daughter while yelling out to the nurse, "What's going on? What's happening to my daughter?"

She didn't answer me but instead expressed to the person she was on the phone with, "He is a crazy a_ _ man and he better stop yelling at me." Referencing me!

She did not get off her phone or stop eating to assist me! I was feeling every emotion rush through my body! I immediately began to assess my daughter's situation. I was calling 911 on one phone and my wife on the other. I traced my daughter's vent tubing to see if there was a puncture. I checked for disconnections and tried to unblock Deonc's airway while describing my emergency to the 911 dispatcher! Deonc's saturations were reading an elevated heart rate and decreased oxygen that were both life ending indications. Deonc has a partial chest plate and partial rib cage. At that moment she needed CPR and chest compressions! In her case, doing that the traditional way, due to her anatomy, could kill her! The nurse gave no assistance of any kind. I worked on my daughter. I gave her mouth to mouth, massaged her chest with my four fingers, and used her ambu bag to stop her lungs from collapsing. I did not know they had already collapsed, but I continued giving my all until my wife, the EMT's, police, and firefighters arrived! I had a choice to react or respond. I chose to respond and reflect on the teachings of care that both my wife and I had to learn at the hospital from the medical team before our daughter could be released to come home. Those teachings are what prepared us to save our daughter's life in case an emergency like this were to ever occur.

The pain of seeing my daughter in that condition still haunts me to this day but the pain also pushed me into lifesaving action. Pain will let us know how we measure up in life. When we identify those areas that need improvement, we can make the necessary adjustments. Had I continued the practice of Reacting by adding the letters (AL) to the end of the word emotion, I would have directed my energy and focus towards being argumentative with the nurse, which could have cost my daughter's life. Instead, I chose the practice of Responding. Because of this and the grace of our HEAVENLY FATHER, our daughter will be sixteen in September.

She is the longest living person with the severity of her syndrome. Many of us run from PA!N because we think it's there to hurt us but once we dissect our pain, dig inside of it with our right and our left hand we're going to feel something. When we pull it out, we'll receive our gift. When we share our gift, we become the very thing that we received, the gift.

For fifteen years I've witnessed my daughter push through the devastating winds just to experience life's simplest joys. Every six months, going through invasive surgery just to keep her alive. It's been well over ten years since she's been undergoing this life prolonging procedure. As a family, all five of us move as one, no matter the category or strength of the storms. In life pain will be a part of the process. Embrace it, dissect it, learn from it, and make adjustments. Discover your gift and continue becoming. All we must do is activate our faith and walk in it. It's God's promise to us that we can do all things through Christ who strengthens us.

GO GET !T<br>
GOD bless

## ABOUT THE AUTHOR:

Social Media:
**Email** fullability1@gmail.com

Darius N. Bradley Sr. currently resides in Fresno Tx. but was born and raised in New Orleans, LA. He is a loving husband and a proud father of three. He is a passionate encourager and speaker.

Bradley is the CEO and co-owner of Full Ability Clothing, an organization advocating for our differently-abled community. He is an aspiring actor, he has featured in music videos and independent film projects. Darius has served his gift of encouragement within the public schools in the Houston metropolitan area.

He has provided team-building activities for national corporations such as Costco, Walmart, Panda Express, and many others. Bradley has provided motivational coaching services for Semi-pro football leagues, local organizations, hospitals, and more.

He does daily motivational videos on all of his social media platforms in addition to composing, editing, and doing voiceovers. He provides daily life coaching support for many community members, family, and friends.

# RT MORGAN
**Derrick Pearson**

Some names are given. Some are assumed. The best ones are earned. There can only be one "Pop."

My story is one that is far too familiar. A person comes along and decides to make your life better by being in it. Better is not grand enough. Best. A person comes along and decides to make your life best by being in it. There was a choice. He could have chosen to do what others have done. He could have ignored the opportunity and moved on. He decided to plant himself firmly in my life and grow the both of us, together. For better and then best.

Roland Thomas Morgan is "Pops." I used the name "Pops" instead of dad or father because the truth is that he is not my DNA father, nor is he my dad. He is that to others and they are blessed for it. As a matter of fact, he shared his kids with me, and they remain as love in my life to this day. "Pops" was the man who day one in my life chose to add to my life, purposefully and pridefully. He chose.

I was eleven or so, and as an abandoned son, I was resistant to giving people credit when it had not been earned. This grown man sitting at my dining room table eating a grown man's breakfast on a Saturday morning had not earned it in my mind. Not being willing to give that respect, I asked one of my favorite questions, "Who are you?"

He told me that I should introduce myself before asking such a thing. That led to a conversation of two bullheaded males, one eleven years old, and another, this grown man. What happened at that dining room table was a ramming of heads over ideas and concepts. It ended in a place of mutual respect and a promise that we each wanted the same thing. We wanted my mother happy and to do so, we promised to be respectful of each other. We became a club of mutual respect of two, and because of this we could reach an agreement on most things going forward. My response was "Okay, Pops!"

Some forty-four years later, that eleven-year-old was searching for information on who my biological father was. It had been emotionally exhausting to track, chase, stalk, pursue, and investigate who this person was. I decided to journal the process. In doing so, certain parts of my history were brought to mind through memories and flashbacks. These memories were in my heart as well as my mind. I battled with the idea that since I was blessed with a pop, maybe it was disrespectful to pursue my father. I did want to know my father's name and face, his story and ours. I also wanted to be sure that I had room in my heart for him and pops, together.

I understood the difference between creating me and raising me. I could not be here at all without my father, and I wouldn't be who I am without Pops. As thankfully as possible, I chose to pay tribute to them both. As I write this, I am in tears. They both are with me. I could not be more grateful.

This man, "Pops", was Roland Thomas Morgan. An American hero. A war veteran disabled with a lost thumb, but not handicapped one bit. He was the manliest man I had ever met. If it could be built, he could build it. If it could be fixed, he could fix it. And if it were funny, he would make it funnier by his laughter.

My mother raised me and taught me how to be a good person. Pops taught me how to be a good man. I know that he was flawed and imperfect. We all are, but he lifted me up in ways that stick with me even today. He challenged me. He inspired me. He supported me. He gave me direction, wisdom, and a helping hand whenever he saw that I really needed it. He gave me love.

He was my personal driver and my personal stylist. He was my favorite deejay and my most respected food critic. He was my co-conspirator in some of the greatest pranks ever, and some of the best birthday surprises and Christmas gifts. He convinced me to not ride the free school bus because I once got in trouble for something that I didn't do. He wanted to protect me from the mean people of the world, but he also just wanted my company. He wanted to pick my brain about the lessons I learned at school. He wanted to learn about today's music and the sports heroes I followed. He wanted to know about my new friends, black and white, and what my dreams were. He had amazing listening skills. He was also a great talker.

He shared his childhood, his dreams, (fulfilled or not) and his passions. He waged a forever battle to get me to like chitterlings and pigs' feet. He lost this battle. I smile just thinking about his sales pitches. "Will put hair on your chest like mine!" (I never got that chest hair and I know that he Is in heaven laughing about it!) He engaged my love for music and expanded it. I cannot listen to Teddy Pendergrass, Eddie Kendricks, Marvin Gaye, or Smokey Bill Robinson without smiling, because of those car rides. I can hear him in our tiny kitchen singing "Is you is or is you ain't my baby..." and doing that weird duck and grind dance along with it. I miss that dance.

Pops made me a boxing fan. He would share tales of Sugar Ray Robinson, Jack Johnson, Jack Dempsey, Joe Louis, and Rocky Marciano. He was by my side as we both cheered Cassius Clay, Muhammad Ali, Joe Frazier, and Sugar Ray Leonard. One of my favorite memories is when my job introduced me to Heavyweight Champion of the world, Riddick Bowe. Bowe held a press conference at my bar and gave me two tickets to see him fight at RFK Stadium in DC. I surprised Pops by asking him to drop me off at the stadium, and then dragged him in for our ringside seats. The time of our lives. We had signed pictures and gloves from the champion. They sat on his dresser forever.

He also loved baseball. He fed my love for Joe DiMaggio and the Yankees. He was mad that I didn't get to see the young Mickey Mantle, but would scream about Jackie Robinson, Willie Mays, and Hank Aaron. Pops would drive us to Baltimore to see the Orioles play at Memorial Stadium. The rides to and from were some of the best conversations. We followed the Orioles from Memorial to Camden Yards, and I loved every minute of it.

He became my favorite fan. He would sneak to my high school games and would try not to let me know. He would slip the next week on the rides to school by telling me to take more shots, stop running out of bounds, and try hitting to right field instead of pulling the ball. This giant of a man would hide behind trees or try hiding in the crowds at my games. He always had some wonderful post-game meal for me. That mattered so much.

He would take me clothes shopping, and this was important. Pops looked good in anything and everything. In the days of shirts unbuttoned to the belly button, he pulled it off. He just looked good in everything. He would laugh at parachute and hammer pants. He loved it when I wore the schools jerseys, and he would check the seam on the jeans I ironed each day before school. "Sharp as a tack!" he would yell! "Seem so tight I could cut my finger on it!" I still envy his ability to grow and beard in full. The man had the magic face.

He shared with me his love for live music. He also shared with me his love for comedy albums. He would buy them and sit me down to introduce the comedians to me as people. There was Moms Mabley, Bill Cosby, and this young cat named Richard Pryor. (Don't let your mom know that I let you listen to him!) In the days of eight-track players, full vinyl albums, and cassette tapes, we would jump in the car, drive to DC and sing as loudly as we could. We would stop by our favorite spot, THE BROILER PIZZA AND SUBS, or we would go to McDonalds and sit in the car with Sister Sledge blaring and burgers being demolished.

He also introduced me and my friends to some of his friends, Johnny, Jack, and Jim. Johnny Walker. Jack Daniels. Jim Beam. He built this bar into the wall in one of the rooms he added to the house. He put a lock on it for appearance's sake, but I had a key, and he knew about it. My friends would stop by, and we would pour some into coke cans then head out for our evenings in Georgetown to dance clubs. He would wait until I got home safely before he would go to sleep.

Pops made sure that I made my bed, washed my clothes, ironed them, and worked out. He made sure that I had a strong work ethic. I delivered papers most of my childhood, and he managed me like he was my boss. Every paper delivered on time, and in place. He got me a summer job that was the hardest thing I have ever done in my life. A company that removed the large demolition trash from buildings in DC. It seemed like we were on the tar roof of every building, and it was one hundred degrees every day. It was so miserable that I couldn't wait for two a day summer football practices to start. They were easy compared to that job!

He determined early that I was smart. He stressed that I better get good grades because I was built for business, not for labor. "Use your brain and not your muscles!" I was horrible at the manual labor that he excelled at. He would laugh at my attempts to use a hand saw or lay brick. I hated it. But he turned that paper route into three. He always checked my work. He never criticized. He managed to weave our conversations to lesson points without ever letting on that he was teaching me, and he was happy to help.

He was my dating voice of reason. He was never wrong about who I should keep dating and those I should run from as soon as possible. He spotted my wife early, even giving her the name "Bex" (short for Rebecca because she was too cool for BECKY) I still use that nickname thirty-five years later. He was protective in the best way ever, always rooting for and cheering for the best in me, for me. He loved out loud.

He shared the best of himself to help me identify the best in myself. He did this until the day he passed away. He never wavered in his love for me, or those who I loved. He never once failed to celebrate my victories or allowed me to wallow in my defeats. I will never forget the day he threw down the gauntlet and challenged my manhood. He noticed my workouts in the basement and said that I was getting too grown to be home. This big 6'3" two-hundred-forty-pound man demanded we go toe to toe. After I bested him, he hugged me and wouldn't let go. He was proud. He was happy. I was grown. I was ready for the world.

I remember one day I came home from Charlotte years later. I had moved there to do a television show with the Carolina Panthers. He and mom had gotten a satellite tv so they could watch my show each week. They taped them all and shared them with neighbors and family. He met me at the door and said, "that brain of yours" and started crying. All two-hundred-forty-pounds of him. And we celebrated in the best way we knew. A shot of Johnny Walker Black.

It is with tears running down my face that I type this. He deserves these tears. It didn't matter what I found out from my DNA dad; he was my 'POPS!' What do you say to someone who comes into your life and makes it better and then best? The three things that I say most in life. Thank you. Love you. Well done!

As I look up to heaven, I say.
THANK YOU, POPS!
LOVE YOU!
WELL DONE!

## ABOUT THE AUTHOR:

Social Media:
**LI** @derrick-pearson-b5580524
**Website** https://www.loveprints.us/
**Email** pearsonderrick@aol.com

Derrick Pearson- Sports Radio Station Owner KNTK-FM Lincoln, Nebraska. Co-Host "Old School with Jay Foreman" "DP One on One" at 93.7 The Ticket FM Lincoln, Nebraska. Speaker-TEDxLander May 2019. The love Project Speaker-TEDxDeerPark March 2020. An American Face 3X Amazon Best Selling Author "The Impact of Influence, (Volumes 1&2) Rebuilt Through Recovery

Derrick "DP" Pearson brings his unique brand of energy to The Ticket's programming and direction. DP has spent stops during his career as a sportscaster, radio and television host, writer, manager, and high school coach. That career has taken him nationwide, including Washington, DC, Charlotte, Los Angeles, Salt Lake City, and Atlanta. In addition to his media and coaching ventures, he also helped establish Fat Guy Charities in Charlotte, an NFL Charity, and developed LovePrints, a national mentor program that promotes Loving and Learning through Sports. DP joins Jay Foreman every weekday from 8:00 am – 10:00 am. One on One with DP airs weekdays from 10:00 – 11:00 each weekday morning.

## THE CHISEL IN MY JOURNEY
### Dr. Jeannie Meza-Chavez

La siento (I feel her). La escucho (I hear her) in every word I speak and every action I take. Ana Maria Meza, mi madre, con raices Mexicanas (Ana Maria Meza, my mother, with Mexican roots). Through her, I carry on the proof that those blessed with the courage to cross borders bring a strong work ethic, purpose, and unwavering faith. From a young age, I recall her tenacity. Whatever it was, she was going to get it done. My mother took a cincel (chisel) from her native Chihuahua, Chihuahua, Mexico, and came to the United States of America para el sueño Americano (for the American dream).

Like many people, she crossed a hostile border. She entered a country that conditions immigrants to believe they are never really American, even when they follow the process to become a U.S. Citizen and doing the manual labor jobs that some tenured Americans will not do. There is judgment in the humble work and defensive English language used. While living in California, my mother cleaned homes for doctors. She also worked in a factory, building camper tops for trucks. I saw my mother work numerous jobs throughout my childhood. She worked a lot.

Her skills as a salesperson were remarkable. She sold Princess House Crystal, Tupperware, Kitchen Fair, Mary Kay, Stanley, and Jafra. I can still picture her getting ready to do the sales demonstrations. She would say, "Una mujer debe siempre dar su mejor desempeño, tener un buen cepillo, perfume, medias, un par de zapatos limpios y estar presentable (A woman should always do her best, have a good brush, perfume, stockings, a clean pair of shoes, and be presentable). This part of the chisel carving taught me about career opportunities I did not want. I wanted to be the person who could afford to buy the products in the beautiful catalogs. I enjoyed flipping through the catalogs. However, as I got older, I learned I'm not particularly eager to shop.

While my sisters and I were in high school, we sold Reese's peanut butter cups, chocolate candy, caramelos (caramel), and assorted Mexican candy. You better believe that when I taste some of those candies now, I am instantly transported back to the journey my mother helped foster. Her skills were evident. My mother was good at being a salesperson. She provided opportunities for my sisters and me to understand the value of work and earning money. Perfect for the environment we were in as our extra-curricular activities at Ysleta High School in El Paso, Texas, always had fundraising attached. Yes, we were the Meza girls whose mother would make enchiladas or tamales for sale without flinching. It was doable. These food sales would provide the profits to travel for a band trip competition to Florida. My mother made sure we had our first experience on an airplane, even if she had to make tamales and enchiladas every weekend.

Let me tell you about the woman I called Mama (Mother). I called her Pariente (Relative). The sacrifices she made on her journey helped create opportunities for me. She helped answer and nurture my questions. I asked a lot of questions. She gave me my first thought and choice in considering careers. You see, the questions I asked led to answers and more questions. In between, my passion grew.

She would say, "Estas buena para abogada" (You are suitable to be an attorney).

I know she was filling me with the opportunity to imagine. At a young age, I did not understand what attorneys did, but she told me. She pointed to the attorneys on her nightly telenovela (soap opera). She watched those Spanish soap operas like missing one episode would put her behind on the big family drama. The soap operas were an extension of our family. I distinctly recall her talking about the soap opera characters as if I should know who these people were. My mother knew the names of all the actors and why they were perfect for the role they were playing. From that, I learned about the complicated lives that these professional actors lived. Somehow, they were still able to put on convincing performances. These nightly, spectacular performances pulled family members to engage in this nightly ritual. Everyone except me is fond of telenovelas (soap operas).

On any given day, the music would blare. It was in Spanish, and it was loud. Just imagine my sisters and me counting to three and synchronizing our exit off her blue station wagon. She was the parent with the loud music driving up to the school slowly so she would not have to make a second round. One of my favorite songs is called La Malagueña, which many artists have interpreted in Spanish, often accompanied by a Mariachi ensemble. Upon listening to the entire song, you identify that it is about a beautiful girl who rejects a man's love because he is poor. Some of the lyrics are as follows:

Malagueña salerosa
Besar tus labios quisiera
Besar tus labios quisiera

Malagueña salerosa
Y decirte niña hermosa
Eres linda y hechicera
Eres linda y hechicera
Como el candor de una rosa
The translation is as follows:
salty malagueña
I would like to kiss your lips
I would like to kiss your lips

salty malagueña
And tell you beautiful girl
you are cute and charming
you are cute and charming
Like the candor of a rose

I recall listening to this song growing up. My mother loved to sing it. Sometimes she sang with mariachi, and other times she sang acapella. I must have been twelve years old when I asked my mother what this song meant. She said, "Los hombres piensan que se trata de algo que les sucede, pero quiero que sepas que se trata de ti; eres hermosa y encantadora, pero nunca te engañes." The translation is (Men think it is about something that happens to them, but I want you to know that it is about you. You are beautiful and charming but don't ever deceive yourself.) When you hear this song's many ranges and variations, you appreciate the passion and purpose of those who accept the challenge to interpret it.

Mom carried her chisel. She added language and perseverance to her toolbox while conserving her culture and love for music. I need more than one chapter to share the impact my mother made and continues to make on me. With her passing on February 2, 2018, I inherited her chisel. Whether I wanted it or not, her passing added a physical finality. She tried to prepare my sisters and me for this moment. Nothing prepares you for the loss of a parent.

For instance, I learned that regardless of the work, I needed to be aware of systems that would attempt to keep me out. Recently, I was asked how I could do the job as a superintendent when the superintendency is predominantly filled with male counterparts. Simple, if there is not an empty chair waiting for me to sit and participate, I build it. My strong work ethic is an inherited trait. When I look in the mirror, I see her. Of all of my sisters, I am the one that looks most like mom. I embrace the compliment because I come from a woman who made it possible for my journey to be what it is today.

I have the chisel, and every day I have the opportunity to begin the day being thankful for the divine purpose I am living. If you had told me I would serve children as a superintendent while growing up, I would not have believed it. I am an advocate for children. I exist to make their learning environment filled with love, hope, and a belief that all things are possible with an education. Education has allowed me to live the American dream beyond my mother's wildest dreams. My mother's impact is evident in the work as I can see myself in the children I serve. I see them, and I feel their struggle.

I have my chisel in my daily work, which includes my native language, Spanish. I am blessed to read, write, and speak Spanish and English. Along with other passionate colleagues, we contribute to creating a system that values the language students talk and reassure them that the language they bring with them is appreciated.

The chisel I choose to use in my daily work is also about my family. I am raising two boys that are blessed beyond measure. I want them to know that we stand on the shoulders of those who have helped carve a space to belong, be of service, and pay it forward. I can do the work I do because I have the support of my husband and family.

I am thankful that my eldest sister sought higher education and carved a path that made it possible for me to see and engage in receiving a bachelor's. I am the first in my family to earn a master's and a doctorate. I have a responsibility to help others in my family and anyone I encounter to become familiar with the possibilities of higher education. Despite my higher learning, the most important lessons came from Ana Maria Meza. Mom degreed me to persevere. Regardless of the hurdles she faced, she kept forging forward.

It has been my firm faith that has pulled me through despite the difficult moments. In my work, I have witnessed the success my students have achieved. I have had the opportunity to see students graduate from college and raise families. Many of my students and their parents have reached out to me to say thank you. Unfortunately, I have also experienced loss in my daily work. I have had my heart broken by the loss of students through accidents or suicide. It hurts.

My daily work is impacted because we have a divine purpose, and it is up to us to honor it.

My childhood memories inspire me. I know that preserving my culture was not as important then as it is now. It is ok for the color of my skin to be what it is. It is brown. It is ok to sound different. People say I have an accent. It is ok for me to pause before speaking because my mind is trying to figure out what language I should use. I come from a place where we cross borders and jump walls because we want what every human being wants, and that is a better life. My culture has prepared me to be in a place where it is up to me to keep carving the space to belong and help bring others on my journey.

As of the time of this writing, I am the first woman from El Paso to serve as President-Elect for the Texas Council of Women School Executives (TCWSE). TCWSE is a state organization committed to empowering women to be better versions of themselves and engaging in helping women prosper and break barriers. Why is this work important? Proverbs 27:17 states, "As iron sharpens iron, so one person sharpens another." My mother spent her life sharpening my sisters and me. Because a woman invested in me, I carry the tremendous responsibility to help sharpen other women. Early in my career, my mentors were men. It was the men that encouraged me. Women must be consistent about promoting and celebrating other women. If you are in a place where this is not happening, pull your chisel out and start carving out a space for women. For clarity, I have also mentored men. There is a place for all of us. Remember, we all have a divine purpose.

In addition, I am the first individual from El Paso to be nominated and selected Regional Superintendent of the Year in 2017 by the Tornillo Independent School District and in 2022 by the San Elizario Independent School District. Two different Boards saw merit in my work ethic. If this work were easy, many would have made this distinction regardless of gender. Yet, I carry this standard of excellence. Children deserve people in the superintendency who make it about children, and not about themselves. What does it mean to be honored for my work as a superintendent? Well, it means that

I have learned about being a teacher for adults to be able to do the necessary work for children. We have heard that some people need to know how to do hard better. Me, I do hard better, and then I take it to the next level. I can do this because the work is not about me, it is about the children I serve every day.

In my daily work, the love of music has empowered me to focus on finding opportunities to bring music to the children I serve. The San Elizario Independent School District has invested in music teachers and instruments. One of my proudest moments is the beginning of the Mariachi Aguila at San Elizario High School. Like many of my students, I grew up listening to mariachi music and have an appreciation for the regional music that continues from generation to generation. Music anchors me. I was one of those children who traveled back and forth to Mexico to attend posadas (pilgrimages) during Christmas and weekend palenques (festivals), all of which included music. Music helps soothe the difficult moments we encounter. That is why my work in this area is important. All of us deserve to carry music in our hearts. For me, it is a fundamental equity issue.

The border that was crossed so long ago was meant to be challenged. My mother's journey taught me about sacrifice and choices. Along the way, I have met individuals who have mentored and inspired my choices. Because of the chisel my mother carried on her journey, she helped me shape the type of chisel I utilize. The chisel I carry carves love, kindness, humility, and a path dedicated to service. Every day, the chisel in my journey is the sweetest reminder of where I come from and what I carry. Mi camino lleva con orgullo un cincel fomentado por la sangre mexicana de mi madre (My journey proudly carries a chisel fostered by my mother's Mexican blood). I feel her love especially on cloudy, rainy days. I hear her saying "Manos a La Obra (Let's Do This)."

## ABOUT THE AUTHOR:

Social Media:
**Email** jeanniemeza@yahoo.com

Dr. Meza-Chavez is married to Dr. Jesus Chavez and is the mother of two boys, Emmanuel and Isaiah Chavez, and a step-parent to Matthew Chavez. Her mother is Ana Maria Meza and father, Alberto Meza. Her siblings are Sandra Luevano, married to Jaime Luevano, Albertina Rodriguez, married to Ronaldo Rodriguez, and Janet Meza, her twin sister.

She is the San Elizario Independent School District (SEISD) superintendent and has approximately 25 years of service as an educator. She holds a Ph.D. in Curriculum & Instruction from New Mexico State University, a Master's in Education / Mid-Management from Sul Ross State University, and a Bachelor's in Creative writing with a Minor in Communications from the University of Texas at El Paso.

She has been selected as the ESC Region 19 Superintendent of The Year in 2022 through her nomination from the SEISD Board of Trustees and once again in 2017 through her nomination from the Tornillo ISD. She has also been recognized by the Texas Council of Women School Executives (TCWSE) as the Region 19 Bravo Award for Exemplary Practice and Innovation and received the Pat Shell Award for Professional Development. In 2013, she received the BEST (Better Educators for Schools in Texas) Scholarship from University of Texas of The Permian Basin.

Dr. Meza-Chavez is a member of the Texas Association of School Administrators (TASA), where she serves on the Membership Committee. She is also a member of the TCWSE where she serves as President-Elect of the state organization. In addition, she is a member of the El Paso TCWSE local chapter. She is also a member of the Texas School Public Relations (TSPRA) and the National School Public Relations Association (NSPRA), where he has received numerous Star Awards for her collaborative work with the San Elizario ISD Public Relations team.

Some of her published work includes the Fall 2021 Communication Matters Magazine for TSPRA's Official Quarterly Digital Publication entitled El Día De Los Muertos, a coauthored article with Ms. Blanca Ivonne Cruz entitled Positive Culture Demands Action: A Latina Leadership Perspective on School Culture published in the Journal of Texas Women School Executives Volume 8, Issue 1., and a 2007 publication in the Journal of Border Educational Research, Volume 6, Number 2 Technology Use of College Bound Seniors from a Southwest Border Community: Preparation, Selection, and Application to College coauthored with Dr. David Rutledge. She was also featured in the ATPE News November 2020 issue A Hot Spot for Connectivity Problems by Sarah Gray.

Her passion for education is contagious, and her energy pushes all to go the extra mile for students. She leads by example with her philosophy of serving to improve the lives of children. She always encourages collaboration and is most enthusiastic when educators transform students' learning environments. She naturally inherited the mantra from conversations with her mother during her upbringing: "Manos a La Obra / Let's Do This."

## MY 2 ROLE MODELS
**Kenneth Wilson**

My early childhood and early adult years were shaped by the two most important men in my life. My grandfather and my father. I am blessed to have had two black men in my life, even though they lived different lives and walked very different paths.

My grandfather is the greatest man I've ever known. He has always been my embodiment of a real man. He was the unquestioned patriarch of our family. He was the person we all turned to for guidance, advice, money, handyman work, and discipline. He was very wise and was able to communicate with confidence and love. He was also a well-respected man in the community. People spoke very highly of my grandfather. I would see other men come by the house to talk with him and ask for his opinion on matters. He was the hardest working man I've ever met. He would get up and go to work almost every day. I spent my summers working at the car dealership with him. Even at work, he received respect and praise from his boss and co-workers. I never heard anyone dare to speak bad about that man.

He was a tall and handsome man. He was a strong and proud black man, with a hint of Native American roots. Even though he worked with his hands, he cleaned up real nice when going out or going to church. He wore a suit well, with nice shoulders and a tall frame. His skin and hair were always groomed. He smelled like excellence.

In his downtime he found time for music and the gospel band he started. He taught himself to play the guitar and sing. Even though he was busy, he always found time for his family. We would eat meals together, take vacations, and go to church. When he wasn't around, we still felt his presence.

As a child I would watch my grandfather in awe. I would hang on to every word he said, even if he wasn't talking to me. I would mimic his walk and his hand movements when he spoke. As a teenager I wanted to be just like him and do everything just like him. He was my role model. I used the same cologne and grooming products. I tried to play baseball because my grandfather played in the Negro Leagues (I wasn't good at baseball, so I played other sports.) I became interested in music. Ultimately, I wanted my grandfather to be proud of me. I sought his approval and blessing in everything I did. One of my most nervous moments was taking my first college visit with him. I wanted my grandfather to like the college more than I wanted to go there.

My other role model was my father. I still call him a role model, but in a very different way. My father wasn't around for most of my childhood and early adulthood years. He had his demons, and unfortunately, they spilled onto the family. My parents separated when I was still young. He would visit occasionally, but most of those visits ended horribly. My parents often fought which led to a toxic environment of violence, abuse, and trauma.

My father was also a tall handsome man. I look like him. He also had a presence about him and a lot of personality. Sadly, I didn't want to remember things he said. He could be very mean and say hurtful things. My father knew how to piss people off and press their buttons. He did not have a very good reputation. Family members would tell wild stories of his antics and shenanigans. He was considered the life of the party, but that party would often end with fighting and arguing.

As I grew up, I despised my father. I barely spoke to or saw him, even though we lived in the same county. When we did speak, he made false promises and never followed through on anything. It wasn't until I started playing sports that he would come to my games, because we had that in common. I tried to teach myself how to block out the pain from not having my father around, but it never worked. I just became numb.

The words, behaviors, and actions of these two men have and will forever shape who I am. Both of their positive and negative influences equally impacted my life. Naturally, the lessons I learned from my grandfather served as a guide for me. He was a clear and positive example of how to conduct yourself as a man. From my father I learned what not to do. I knew that I didn't want to be like him, because I already had an excellent example of the right way in my grandfather.

As an adult, I have come to appreciate the hard lessons I learned from my father. By revealing the wrong path, he allowed me to navigate life without making those same mistakes. I was extremely motivated to never become like him. I had a real-life example of how bad decisions would affect my life. Those lessons proved to be just as valuable as the lessons I learned from my grandfather.

Over time I have been able to forgive my father for the pain and trauma he caused me and the rest of the family, though it did not come easy. It started with therapy, as I attempted to understand my anger towards my father. I wanted to just forget him and let go, but I was not able to. That anger was beginning to build inside of me and affect other areas of my life. It was extremely hard to be around people that reminded me of him. I struggled in social settings where alcohol was served, because I hated alcohol and people that drank. I felt myself becoming consumed by these feelings and emotions. I needed help. Therapy allowed me to see my father (and grandfather) as human beings. I learned they were trying to figure out life just like everyone else. Both men made mistakes, and also had triumphs. I remember the good qualities of both men. I also have positive memories from both. As I continue to age and mature in my own life, I gain more clarity and understanding of theirs.

I have been able to turn the negative memories and experiences into positive lessons. It has given my father's life a renewed purpose to me. He did teach me a lot, it just didn't come in the traditional methods. Those lessons have allowed me to dig deep and understand my own personality, actions, and motivations. I have learned so much about my own behaviors and cognitive psychology. Through the good and the bad, I would not be the man today without my father's lessons.

I learned that it is easy to admire "good" people. The reality is we are all humans with challenges and struggles that may not be seen on the surface. Everyone's life has value. We should not be so quick to judge or dismiss people, and the value they can bring to your life.

As a husband, father, and mentor I can share the lessons received from my grandfather and my father. I can speak about both men from a place of honor and respect. Their lessons do not end with me. They have become the foundations of our family legacy.

In memory of my grandfather Robert Robinson Sr., and my father Kenneth Wilson. Thank you for the impact you both had on my life. I promise to continue your legacies and honor you. I love you.

## ABOUT THE AUTHOR:

Social Media:
**LI** @kennethrwilson1
**Website** www.kennethrwilson.com
**Email** kennywilson65@gmail.com

Kenneth R. Wilson is a native of Silver Spring, MD. He is a proud husband and father of three children. Kenneth had worked in the fields of nonprofits, business, education, and local politics. He worked hard to hold positions on every corporate level, from volunteer to Executive Director and Board President. He has also worked with individuals, groups, and families of all ages and ethnicity groups. For years Kenneth has been a passionate and active member in the community, serving as a mentor, voice, and a connector in the community.

With his organization Men of Stature, Kenneth works with Black Men providing support and safe spaces in the areas of health, virtue, and fellowship. Men of Stature also provides mentoring to youth, and programs to promote literacy in the black community.

Kenneth's passion as a community health expert provides instruction and advocacy on safety and other life saving measures. He believes in the importance of helping others and learning what to do in emergency situations.

Kenneth's voice and thoughts can be heard on several shows and podcasts including The Positive Isn't Popular Podcast and The Speakeasy Show.

Accomplishments
- Founder of Men of Stature
- 2016 President's Lifetime Achievement Award Recipient
- Multiple Bestselling Author
- International Community Health Expert & Advocate

## BARRIERS LEADING TO SUCCESS
**Leslie Davis**

I dedicate my story to my late mother. The one who's had an influential impact on my life and story. She played a major part in helping me become the young lady I am today. For that, I am blessed and grateful to have had a mom who was over-protective of her children's abilities. I also want to thank Chip Baker for giving me an opportunity and platform to tell my story.

"For I know the plans I have for you," declares the LORD, "plans to prosper you and not to harm you, plans to give you hope and a future."
- Jeremiah 29:11

My name is Leslie Davis. I am a mother to four beautiful daughters, a wife to a wonderful husband, full time Mentor Manager and Founder/President of a Non-Profit Youth Organization.

I was born in a small town in Texas and raised by both my parents until one of their lives was cut short. A death I did not see coming nor did I understand why I had to experience this type of hurt. Losing a parent at a young age really took a toll on my life. I can honestly say I do not look like what I've been through. The smiles, accomplishments, and positive demeanor is what people witness when they interact with me, but they know nothing about the pain I've endured. I am who I am because I've overcome the obstacles I was dealt. The heartbreak of losing a parent caused me emotional pain and put me in some very dark places. With time I took that hurt and used it as my footstool to climb to a place of healing and prosperity.

I wasn't the type to discuss my problems. I didn't go around spreading my business to everyone. All my battles were fought silently, but in the mist of my sorrow God never lifted his hands off of me. I often questioned my life and God's desire for my future. Through it all, I eventually discovered my purpose in worship and God showed me my purpose in life. Once you find your purpose you'll find strength, inspiration, and strive to fulfill your place here on earth. Just know that when you're doing God's work, you're aiding the people around you and revealing to God your obedience. Know that my journey has not been easy, but as I speak my truth, I find it amazing that healing led me to the prosperity aspect of my life. It may have taken me thirty-six years to find my purpose and tell my story, but remember growth requires time.

"What we suffer now is nothing compared to the glory he will reveal to us later."
- Roman 8:18

My mother Tracey Pittman Cooks battled ovarian cancer for five years. She found out she had cancer at the age of thirty. I wish I could eradicate the pain and suffering I witnessed her endure from my memory. Could you envision being a child watching your mother battle an aggressive sickness? There were days my mother couldn't even get out of the bed or care for her children due to the chemo treatments. I knew my mom was ill, but I didn't fully understand the severity of her illness and how deadly the disease was. I don't recall anyone talking with me or my siblings regarding the progress of my mom's health. Maybe we were too young to comprehend it all, but during the days my mother was sick she had plenty of fight in her. Her strength was unmatched and even with a bald head her beauty was flawless. Her spirit was as bright as the stars. She had a heart of gold and compassion for others. If you ever had an encounter with her, you know just how kind and sweet she was as a person. Beautiful soul inside and out. Everyone who crossed her path was blessed to have known her as a person. Her love for others was shown daily and her presence left a positive mark. As she transitioned over her love and affection for others never faded.

Growing up without my mom was not easy. As an adult it got worse for me because I felt I needed her presence more than I did as a child. Life was not the same without her. I missed her so much. Holidays and birthdays were hard, but Mother's Day was the toughest holiday for me. The void of not having her here with me on that day always put me in a depressed stage. The protection, love and support a mother has for her child could never be replaced or forgotten. I reminded myself of this daily, but I thank God for prayer and healing. Mother's Day of 2020 I prayed and asked God for comfort to heal and find strength in accepting the fact that my mother transitioned to a better place, and I no longer had access to her presence. The pain and loss became so unbearable. I had no choice but to turn to God for comfort because I was slowly losing myself. The unknown version of myself hit rock bottom and the only way I was going to find myself was to heal. That's when I began to focus on the positive mark my mother left on the earth before her departure. The beauty, kindness, and warm heart. Having her for ten years of my life was just enough time for me to remember what was left of her and what it meant for me.

It may have taken me years to understand why God chose me to be the motherless child, but I am grateful that he revealed my purpose to me. Although our time spent together was short, she inspired me to be who I am today and impacted me in a major way.

My mother aided my developmental milestones as a child. She made sure my siblings and I exceeded expectations in school and at home. She wanted the best for us, and education was her top priority. One of her wishes was for us to finish high school. Under no circumstances were we to ever drop out. She preached the importance of finishing high school and getting a high school diploma, but to me that accomplishment wasn't enough. I felt the need to go harder and not just stop there. I did as my mother requested, but that wasn't enough for me. I had to continue making her proud, so I received my Associate and Bachelor's degree in Business. I became the Founder and President of a Non-Profit Youth Organization called A Reason to Dream. My siblings and I were held to a certain standard. My mom had high expectations for us. I am blessed to say my mother Tracey Pittman Cooks conquered her role of transforming me into the beautiful young lady she expected and knew I would be. My mother's influence contributed to my character and ability to adjust to life. Her impact and love will last for a lifetime.

> "For everything, there is a season and a time for every matter under heaven."
> - Ecclesiastes 3:1

Witnessing my mother battle ovarian cancer taught me to never underestimate the strength of a woman. Women are superior, we were born to be strong even when we feel our lowest. We hide and cover up the pain just to keep pushing for the ones we love and support. As my late mother did for me. I vow to do the same for my family and the community. My mother fought till she couldn't fight any more. She gave it her all and I witnessed her strive. Her devotion to her family was remarkable and for that I vow to apply pressure in all endeavors of life. Her battle taught me to never be weak, but to stand on faith and God's promise. This led me to release the strong hold of my mother's absence and stand on strength.

Healing from my past led to my vision of starting a Youth Non-Profit Organization which supports the community by offering educational trainings, workshops, camps and programs that support positive youth development.

The mission statement is to promote healthier life skills, increase education skills and build character in young people to help them sustain a successful life.

The vision statement is to build confidence, deliver hope and present opportunities.

A Reason to Dream organization has provided over three hundred kids the tools needed to be great leaders, look beyond their imagination, and Dream Big. The youth are encouraged to shape their boldest dreams into reality and presented new skills and opportunities to become successful. My goal as a community leader is to protect, heal, and manifest the spirit of the community through our programs.

If there is a child who is experiencing a hard time at school or home, as a community leader I want to give them the opportunity to turn their pain and grief into something positive. To teach them that no matter what the circumstances are, you take your life lessons, heal, and find strength to overcome the barriers.

A Reason to Dream is vital to the community because it helps bridge the gap between school and home. Our focus is to ensure kids are still learning outside of the traditional classroom. We offer kids the opportunity to receive certifications and leadership roles that add value to their resumes.

> "Weeping may endure for a night, but joy cometh in the morning."
> - Psalm 30:5

I took my grief and pain and used it to be a blessing to others. I get joy and love out of providing the youth with opportunities. The activities I experienced as a child kept my mind from wandering on the past events in my life. I want to offer the youth the same privileges I had to help overcome trauma. You never know what people are going through. Children normally aren't vocal about their emotional state, as I was when I was younger. If it wasn't for staying busy with activities and camps outside of school as a child, there is no telling where life would have taken me.

I'm happy to say I've found my purpose and have become the best version of myself. The hurt that I had built up was released. I'm now growing into the woman that Gods wants me to be. I was once lost and didn't understand what aspiration or intent God had for me, but he showed up in his timing. God provided me the tools I needed to become a great role model and leader. My four daughters are fortunate to have a mother who provides them the privilege to witness the strength and determination of a wife, mother and businesswoman. I am teaching my girls and the kids in the community what it takes to have strength, love and philanthropy.

I miss my mother dearly and I'm grateful for the precious moments we spent together. I was showered with unconditional love and nourishment. My mother is my greatest inspiration. A wife, mother, and friend gone to soon. Her legacy of love, compassion and strength shall live on through me. She taught me the true meaning of inspiration. Through the Non-Profit Youth Organization and by sharing my life story with others, I hope to motivate others and give them hope and strength during tough times. I want them to understand Gods timing, his purpose and to believe that anything you put your mind to will prevail. As I continue to grow and learn from my peers, I will spread the word of gospel to help others become the best version of themselves. I am beyond blessed to share parts of my admiration and inspiration from my late mother.

## ABOUT THE AUTHOR:

Social Media:
**Email** areason_todream@yahoo.com

Leslie K. Davis is the daughter of Joe Cooks Jr. and the late Tracey Pittman Cooks. She graduated from Hearne High School and received her bachelor's degree in business from the University of Phoenix. Leslie is a Mentor Manager at the Big Brothers Big Sisters of the Brazos Valley. She is the Founder and President of A Reason to Dream, which is a non-profit youth organization.

Leslie devotes her time to her non-profit youth organization A Reason to Dream, where she and her team have provided children in the Brazos Valley Region an opportunity to showcase new skills and interests through the organization.

A Reason to Dream's mission is to promote healthier life skills, improve education skills and build character in young people to help them sustain a successful life.

The organization has impacted over 300 kids by providing educational opportunities, teaching the importance of setting goals, and aiding kids to dream big.

Leslie has always had a passion to serve the welfare of others. Growing up as a child she watched as others cared for her mom who lost her battle with ovarian cancer when Leslie was only 10 years old. As Leslie grew older, she found peace and the strength to allow her mother's legacy to live on through her. Her mother instilled in her the beauty and admiration to be someone who could help change the world around her.

Leslie is also a team member of I Heart Hearne, whose goal is to bring love and unity through community events.

When Leslie isn't working, she enjoys spending family time with her husband Christopher Davis and their 4 daughters.

Leslie's favorite scripture is:

"For with God nothing shall be impossible Luke." - 1:37 (KJV)

# YOUR CIRCLE
**Dr. Lindsie O'Neill Almquist**

Your circle. The people brought in your life that have become your people or have a huge impact on why or how you are. You know those people. They are your influence. They are your celebratory team, your go getters, your person who you text when you need to be real, raw, and authentic. These are the ones that impact us just by their presence. The million mini moments that create who we are and how we continue to give love and light to others is absolutely revitalizing because YOUR life is worth it. You were born for such a time as this. You can be unapologetically who you are. But YOU must believe it. Do it. Reach for it. Focus on it. Be refined in the fire. This is how we are impacted and how we impact others.

I didn't know that the trials of my life, or the people in it, had navigated me to the above-mentioned beliefs, but boy have they. I remember my counselor in middle school, after my parents got divorced, holding me and letting me sit in her office each time I would throw up while trying to open that middle school door. She carried me. She loved me through my down days. She didn't let me think less of myself during those dark times. She is an example of the impact of influence. Give it up to our amazing counselor that has literally saved childrens' lives. <3

During the summer after my eighth-grade year, I met an Interim Superintendent that allowed me to be in the school I went to high school at. He changed the trajectory of my life. His impact in my life was one of the pivotal moves for me to see that educational leadership was something I could see myself as part of. I was unapologetically who I was in high school because I felt that I was in a place that wanted me. He provided that safe place and all kids deserve that. When you feel wanted, welcomed, and loved, you grow. It seems so obvious, but I think we can all agree that common sense is not common.

I remember working three jobs and going to Texas A&M (Whoop!) thinking I couldn't do it. I was taking twenty-one hours a semester and trying to keep it altogether. I took one step at a time. Face it until you make it. Backwards Design. Focus on the goal. Fail forward. Whip it into shape. Get going. I felt that was my strategy to graduate and start teaching. Just do the thing. To be honest, it was one of the hardest parts of my academic journey, and I have a doctorate. I am a hard worker, but boy I'm not great at heavy intense math and it showed. If it weren't for friends, I definitely would not have survived. They sat me up and pushed me forward. Their support of me along with them not allowing me to be consumed by my own self doubt during the tough times were the #1 reason that I finished my undergraduate studies. Friends are, and can be, the rawest form of influence that makes a substantial impact.

Making carrot cake. Ten years ago, at our wedding, I wanted carrot cake. It's not because I am a "carrot top" either. I just wanted carrot cake. I love it and being unapologetically who I am, I couldn't shake the craving for carrot cake. Well, no one really makes inexpensive carrot cake. My sweet, dear best friend, Jessica made the cake. She has always been that best friend that will do whatever she can whenever she can. Watching and walking alongside each other's Momma's trials has been both painful, refreshing, and influential. We met through our babysitter when we were infants and it's been a bond we can't shake (much less want to). People like this: Hold on to them. They are few and far between.

The Ashleys in your life. After I called off my first engagement, I was broken. It was the hardest, smartest decision of my life up until that point. I had a friend Ashley who selflessly let me be authentically raw with pain. I experienced that pain in ways that I had never and have never experienced pain. She walked along that journey. She was kind and yet critical with love. She was the impact of influence in my life that allowed me to make it to the next part of my journey. She was such a blessing and pure joy. We don't see each other much now, but people like this, you can't forget. Ever. They are the lighthouses in the sea gone awry.

The neighbor girls. Where would I be without you? From bringing us hand-me-downs that have clothed my son for most of his young life. You've come to my door and stayed at my house when we needed something. You've laughed with our joys and held us through our shame. You're the best. Your influence in my life of how to be a mom/wife/life friend has upped my level of expectation for good neighbors. The eggs across the fence. Taking dogs out when we need help. The conversations about life and death. The love that you show daily despite whatever is going on. One of them, after our friend's home burnt down, went to Sam's and got them items after only meeting them once. What an influence.

JD. I am not really sure there has ever been a friend in my husband's life, that I have known, that has acted or behaved quite like JD. He is silent, kind, and not really one that I got to know very well, but I knew him. I knew him by the way he was with my husband. I knew him by the things that he would do with and for my husband. He's a strong, gentle soul that always puts others first, helps others out and is always lending a hand. When his newly bought and remodeled family home burnt down, my heart broke for them. I don't think I jumped out of my house with two kids on a Saturday as fast as I did that day. I was at their place in no time. Caring for them has been such an honor and privilege as he has done so much for my sweet husband. His impact of what a man's best friend is has been something I pray every good man has.

2009. I met a group of ladies in 2009. They are a group that's unmatched. They have held me in the lowest of lows and celebrated with me in the highest of highs. They're those people that you know were meant to be your circle. They have been the unsung heroes of my adult life. You cannot make it in this life without people like the 2009 queens. They carry you, push you, make you laugh when all you want to do is cry, and love on your babies. They are a circle you can't believe you have and can't think of being without, even when you aren't able to be with them as much as you want.

The Zaidas of the world. I met Zaida through an extraordinary experience when we applied to go to Harvard for a summer. We got accepted through Raise Your Hand Texas (now Charles Butt Foundation), a wonderful non-profit that elevates public education. I am a people person and I LOVE people. I love meeting new people, learning about their lives and their lived experiences, and just sitting in the presence of others. I am normally a big fan of others and their aspirations. Zaida is calm. The ying to my yang. Her babies are all grown and mine are just starting school. She has never let the reality of where we are in life be a division. Instead, we have soaked up the time together, being just a phone call or text away to support and uplift each other personally or professionally. I am honored to have Zaida in my circle. I remember when we first met. We were at Harvard through Raise Your Hand Texas, an amazing non-profit that supports public education, and she was absolutely precious. (and still is!). Since that day, many moons ago, we have continued to learn and grow alongside each other through programs such as JG Consulting Leadership Academy, a wonderful company for school leaders led by James Guerra. Check it out! It was and still is one the greatest memories of my professional networking experiences post Harvard. Zaida, you are the type of impact that every person deserves to be influenced by. More Zaidas in this world, loving on others, is what we all need and deserve.

How we live, serve and care for others is critical in regard to how your circle is elevated. While I am not close to a ton of people, I think ensuring people feel loved, safe to be who they unapologetically are, and rawly authentic is hands down and one hundred percent what being a person of influence is. I remember the day my friend Jenny (rockstar educational leader by the way) sent me earrings. Just a random act of kindness in the mail. Those earrings have meant more to me than just any old pair ever have or will. The thought, the time, and the moment meant so much. I realized she took the time to think of me and do that in her busy life. It was by far one of those moments where even as busy as we are in schools we find time to be the change we wish to see. Her servant's heart made my days much brighter and helped me continue to fight the good fight.

Connecting people, networking, giving HUGS (yes, I said HUGS ;)). Remember even if it's just for a moment in time your circle matters. How you connect with people matters. All of the moments I have shared with you have shown the power of connection. Networking and being unapologetically who you are provides light for where you should, can and will shine. You don't want to be someone you're not, be with people that don't elevate you, or be around those that don't give hugs. Seriously y'all. Give a darn hug. PEOPLE NEED IT. Those that matter don't mind and those that mind don't matter. If it's something medical, obviously be respectful, but do the darn thing. Love on people. Give life into the world. Your circle is not always chosen by you. Mine at work, during my undergraduate, masters and doctoral programs all have been given to me. They're a gift. Learn from them, allow them to influence you in the ways in which uplift, encourage and motivate you and your calling. After all, we GET to do this. Every stage we are allowed to experience in life, it's a "I get to…" and for that those people within it, soak them up. The people that are meant to continue on your journey will. Remember the Zaidas. They're your circle. They're your influencers that have been the trajectory impact. Not everyone will be that and that's absolutely ok. Just because someone isn't meant for you, doesn't mean they're not meant for someone else. Connect, network, and give the darn hug. YOLO.

Here we are in 2023. Not much has changed since the beginning of time. People matter. People have purpose. People that become your circle are exponentially influential on and in your life. They have profound impact into generations after you. The ability to even have a circle, even if it's just one, one that you can have to trust, grow, and be authentically who you are, is an absolute treasure. My circle, and all of its layers, lend to the person I am today. Without the professional and personal circles and experiences that have been the circles of support along the way, we cannot be who we were meant to be. The team, the network, and your circle matter. Choose it wisely, of course, but aspire to have a multi-faceted circle where people come into your life, and you don't want them to leave because iron is refined in the fire.

## ABOUT THE AUTHOR:

Social Media:
**LI** @lindsiealmquist
**Website** https://sites.google.com/view/drlindsiealmquist
**Email** LindsieAlmquist@gmail.com

Lindsie is a passionate servant leader in the central Texas area. She has served in public schools from elementary to high school in small, six man football rural districts to large urban from teacher to central office roles. She loves traveling, spending time with family and friends, and volunteering. She is a proud fightin' Texas Aggie, Texas State Bobcat and UT at Austin Longhorn. She loves leading, empowering and serving others.

# WHO IS LEADING YOU, AND, WHO ARE YOU LEADING?
**LS Kirkpatrick**

Hello. My name is LS Kirkpatrick. Are you ready to be influenced by me?

Quite a statement and question, isn't it? There is a lot of power in what I asked. Who influences you? Who do you influence? Does it happen conciously, subconsciously, or both? Are you influenced daily or is it a once in a lifetime thing? What does it really mean to be influenced or to influence someone else?

I pondered these questions as I thought about who influenced me in my life. How can I pick just one person, can you? For me, I want to say my grandmother did, but my grandfather was also a balance to her. Then there are my siblings. I was around them and my parents more than anyone else. How did each one influence me, or did they? What about friends, neighbors, or people I met briefly; can they have an impact on my life? Did your friends, neighbors, or people you met briefly have an impact on your life? What about inanimate objects like books, songs, or movies?

Yes, I believe they all can.

When I was growing up, I observed my siblings, what made them happy, sad, angry, and how they interacted with each other. I avoided stressing out about school grades after my eldest sibling came home one day from school sobbing because she got an A- on one paper. I saw how my other siblings tried to comfort her and encourage her. They would have been elated to get an A-. School was more difficult for them in certain subjects. A few days later she finally stopped crying and being sad about it. I was influenced by her and my siblings' interaction to not stress out over one grade you get in school, especially one that was still worth being proud of.

I was influenced by many of my siblings' interactions with each other. The way they responded to each other in each situation helped me choose how I wanted to be.

Have you ever heard a parent say to a child, "Stay away from so and so, they are a bad influence on you?"

I remember one sibling's friend that our mother would say this about. As a child I didn't see what was bad about it, they weren't troublemakers. Now as an adult, I understand the concerns our mother had. One doesn't instantly end up in a life that is not healthy. It is small things, or steps, then one day one might ask, "How did I end up in this situation?" What kind of influence are you to others?

What about cousins and aunts and uncles? One side of our family was happy, caring, and knew how to enjoy each other's company. The other side of our family was not. Some were, but there was always an uneasiness about them. I knew what I did not want to be like because of them. I learned how I did want to be from the others. There are many blended families so there can be many sides of family to be influenced by. What about your family?

I mentioned my grandparents earlier. My grandfather was stern but could laugh. My grandmother was kind and loving but was a fierce competitor. My grandfather seemed scary to me, until one day I was attacked by a cat (which he had told me to not be around, but I did not listen). He scooped me up in his arms, carried me into the house and though he was not happy with me for not listening, he was genuinely concerned about me. I looked at my grandfather differently after that and modeled the good in him.

My grandmother, she played to win, any game that she played. She influenced me to not hold back, to be a gracious winner, a good loser, and to enjoy life in all aspects. She found joy in all things, and taught me how to be a grandmother, though I didn't know it at the time. It is difficult to be a grandparent, to know what your role is and what the parent's role is. When a situation arose, I would think back to how my grandparents handled it, especially disciplinary situations, and followed their example. It proved to be exactly the right thing to do.

Has one statement from someone influenced a change in the path you are taking?

It did for me, twice. I can't even remember who the first one was anymore. It was a one-time encounter. This person said something to my parents that changed the direction of my thinking and my young life forever, in a positive way.

There was another one-time encounter. It was at a rockshop in Madras, Oregon. The gentleman who was talking with us asked me a question. He was showing my family some rocks and opals he got from an expedition that he acquired in Australia. I think I was twelve at the time and said that I wanted to go to Australia one day.

He got down to eye level with me (I was very short at that age still) and he said, "Do you want to go or are you going to go?" I started to answer, and he stopped me and said, "If you want to go, you will never get there. It is a nice thought. But if you say you are going to go and you keep saying that, then you will go."

At the time, I thought that was the strangest thing, then I said, "I am going to go." I studied it, learned about it, and read about it. I totally immersed myself into all I could about Australia. I could tell you anything you wanted to know about it, but my heart was not in it. It was a want, not something that I saw myself doing, except once in a while. To this day I still have not gone. He was right.

I understand now that what he was talking about is called mindset. Like the story of the young man that was a janitor. Each day he saw the diplomas and certificates on the wall of the office building he was cleaning. Each day he saw his own name on them and he was no longer a janitor there. He shared his vision with one whose name was on some of the certificates and diplomas. That man guided him to be able to achieve his dream.

It seems we can influence ourselves to a positive change and success in our own lives.

What does influence really mean? From my searching for the answer, the repeating theme is this: "Influence is the power to have an impact on someone or something." I believe that can mean the influence you have on yourself as well.

As I examined what influence meant, I also saw that an influencer is a leader. Have you ever thought of yourself as a leader? I believe we can lead throughout our lives, even if we do not realize we are doing so.

Some leaders are great and memorable. Others are not. What kind of leader are you? Do you influence positive changes? Do you influence changes in the world? Do you influence correct guidance in your family?

What you may need to ask yourself is this:

What makes a leader great? What do all great leaders do that people want to follow or emulate them? How do leaders influence people without even trying to do so?

Leadership is another topic and for a different book, but not to be lightly dismissed here. Great leaders are great influencers. How they do this is important. Have you ever thought of why they do this? What is their motivation?

If someone comes up to you and says give me money, are you likely to do it? If another person comes up to you and talks about a great cause and the benefits it has for others, are you at least willing to listen? If someone comes up to you and asks how they can serve you today, this week, this month, would you be more inclined to take some time and talk with them?

Leadership, in my humble opinion, is about serving and giving. People want a leader that has their best interest at heart. Leaders influence by example and by caring about the people they interact with. Yes, there have been leaders that were harmful to society, that influenced masses of people to do things that were harmful to others.

What was their influence? What did they promise their followers they would get out of listening to them and acting upon what they had to say?

Did you catch that? What did they offer the people to enhance their own lives? I think it was the influence of what we all want, a better life. Influence should improve the lives of those who are listening to you, watching you, emulating you.

Sometimes you don't even know you are influencing others until one day; someone sends you an email stating how they have been seeing what you do and would like your advice on something. Or someone walks up to you and says something to the effect that they have seen all you do and how you treat other people and they just want to let you know, they are proud of you.

What about inanimate objects? Do books influence you? Do movies, music, news, or other things influence you? We can be influenced by singers, actors, authors, look at the changes in the world over the past hundred years.

As you read these stories of influential impact on lives, think of the impact others have made on your life. Why did you listen to them? What is it you were gaining from what they said or demonstrated that you wanted to include in your own life or in the lives of those around you?

As you read these stories of influential impact on lives, my hope is that you can see the impact you have on those around you. If it is not the impact you want, you do have the ability to change the perspective you have, then change the direction you are taking. This will change the influence that you have on others.

Life is fluid. You can go with the flow, you can go against the flow, or you can create your own flow, but life will continue to flow.

One last thought I would like you to consider.

Who do you know that is a worldwide influencer?

In my parents' time, it was Shirley Temple. She brought innocence and a beautiful smile into a world of war and anguish.

In my time, it was Billy Graham. He brought peace that went to the very core of your being. He also brought clarity into a world of confusion and unrest.

Who is the world influencer in your time? What do they bring to the world? Is it you? You do not have to influence the whole world, but you can influence one person. That one person can influence one or even three others. Of those three, one of them may influence a hundred people. Of those one hundred people, one person may be the one to influence the whole world. That could not have happened if you had not been the one to influence that one other person.

What is your impact of influence?

## ABOUT THE AUTHOR:

Social Media:
**LI** @writers2readers
**Website** https://www.lskirkpatrick.com
**Email** writers2readers@protonmail.com

Author LS Kirkpatrick - after thirty years of family history and research, she decided to write stories for her grandchildren. She is a wife, mother of four, and grandmother of fifteen. Her accomplishments include but are not limited to farming, ranching, an Associates of Science and Associates of Applied Science degrees, over thirty years researching genealogy and DAR member patriots, author of five legacy books, three published books on Amazon; currently in six collaborative book projects. "I gain inspiration from life itself. We are all connected through personal encounters, some are brief, and others are lifelong relationships. I absolutely love what I do; it's very rewarding."

https://www.lskirkpatrick.com

# MY WHY
**Manny Trujillo**

We all have been molded and influenced by the people and events in our lives. Hopefully, our positive influences help us through life and encourage us to positively impact someone else by reciprocating the lessons we learned. When I became a dad over twenty-one years ago, I knew that I wanted to set a positive example for my kids each day. I quickly realized that they were watching my wife, Kandice, and me from the time they were itty bitty, and soaking up information like a sponge. They saw and listened to our interactions with people. They watched how we handled situations. They continue to do so to this day. While we are in no way perfect, we still hope to influence our kids in a positive way through the way we treat others and by the way we approach life circumstances. As a parent, I know that we just want what is best for our children. We want to give them more than we had, but this doesn't necessarily mean material items. I've known many people with overflowing bank accounts that never received the love they were hoping for. While I have spent fatherhood striving to give my kids the love and positive influence they deserve, they have also impacted me in ways that have shaped the person I am today.

I have had the honor of being in The Impact of Influence Series before. Through my previous writing, I gave well deserved flowers to many of my family members and mentors. I was so happy and grateful that the majority of my loved ones were able to read those chapters in front of me because those are priceless moments I will never forget. Through this most recent chapter, there are four people I would like to honor. They are the loves of my life. My pride and joy.

Call me Nostradamus.

As soon as I saw Kandice Hay in her cheerleader uniform that September afternoon at our first junior high football pep rally, I knew, "THAT'S WIFEY RIGHT THERE!" Luckily, I had my cousin, Rudy, as a wingman. I will forever be indebted to him. We started dating later that school year and have been together ever since. Junior high sweethearts are a rarity. We will celebrate our twenty-seventh wedding anniversary this December, and I consider myself the luckiest guy on the planet. I constantly refer to myself as Ray Guy because I know that I outkicked my coverage. She is the perfect partner and is so supportive in everything that I have done. She loves our kids like no other and gives each of them all of her love and caring. Compassion is probably her best trait. While she wants what is best for our children, she won't hand it to them on a silver platter; however, they know without a doubt, she is always in their corner. In addition to her role as a mom, she is an amazing educator. She pushes her students to strive for greatness. Kandice is also a friend that gets called on for advice quite a bit, or just for a listening ear. I feel the most important thing that we have for each other is respect. It makes our relationship work. Our relationship has impacted me by making me realize that relationships which are meant to be make life joyful. We really are like peas and carrots, hot cocoa and marshmallows, and most importantly, like beef stew and cheese rolls. We just go together. I look forward to what our future holds and sharing all of life's upcoming gifts with you. I love you.

Kade Grant

I can still remember when my life changed forever. I was studying for my bus driving certification test. Kandice had worked a full shift and was tired. At around 10 PM she told me she was having some mild contractions, but they were several minutes apart. I went to bed. Kandice woke me up around 1 AM and told me that she thinks her water broke. Her contractions were around five to seven minutes apart. We stayed calm, drove to the hospital and they hooked Kandice up to a fetal monitor. I can still remember the nurse saying, "Let's get you in a room; looks like we are having a baby today."

I called the soon to be grandparents. On July 10, 2001, Kade Grant Trujillo was born. He was such a good baby. We learned on the fly, but he made it easy on us. Watching him grow was a blessing. He was loved by everyone, and was always a people pleaser, wanting to do everything and beyond that was expected of him. I didn't get many opportunities to pick him up from school, but when I did there was always a teacher there to tell me, "Kade is the most respectful young man."

My dad chest would swell with pride. I knew he was watching. Kade was a great athlete and excelled on the soccer field, basketball court, football field, and track. I loved bringing him on the sidelines at the end of a game when I was coaching, and he was still a little guy. He would wait until after the game so he could run the one hundred yards and score a touchdown. It was fun just being his Dad, having the opportunity to sit in the stands and watch Kade and his teammates play. In addition to being an excellent athlete, Kade is very academically goal driven. As a freshman in high school, he made a lofty goal to get into the engineering program at Texas A&M University, his mom's alma mater. Come graduation, Kade was a top ten percent graduate from Klein Collins High School, an all-district football player, and an all-state academic athlete as well. He will probably get embarrassed that I am even putting that information in here. In a time of "look at me", he has never been that guy. I admire that so much; he is a true teammate. That lofty goal that he set for himself as a high school freshman is coming to fruition. Kade is currently completing his junior year at Texas A&M University, majoring in engineering. To say that Kandice and I are proud is an understatement. My relationship with my oldest son has impacted me in so many positive ways, but mainly, I have learned that he represents our family's greatest traits. He has shown me that it's good to be strong and compassionate. While routine and structure are good, it's fun to venture off the path once in a while to see where it will take you. I love you, Kade; I know your life is destined for greatness.

Karson Palmer

Karson has asked many times, "Where did I get my name?" Well, at first, I named Karson because I liked the way it sounded. At the time, Carson Palmer was a very good quarterback for the Cincinnati Bengals. In retrospect though, his name fits him perfectly because it's unique and sets him apart. Anyone who has met Karson will tell you, to know Karson is to love him. He has the kindest, most giving heart and he is an absolute free spirit that marches to his own beat. We waited five years to have our second child.

Karson Palmer Trujillo was born on May 31, 2006. When Karson was born, we thought we would be getting a carbon copy of his brother Kade. Instead, Karson was his own unique little guy with light brown, wispy hair, and a raspy voice. He had a love for imagination and superheroes instead of sports. He couldn't get any cuter; he had everyone in the palm of his hand. We have a lot of "Karson stories" that are repeated time and again because he is a funny truth teller. If you don't want the truth, you might want to think twice about asking him. If he starts tilting his head and scratching the top of his head to ponder what he's going to say, brace yourself because he is going to share his unfiltered thoughts with you.

While Karson is a free spirit and creative thinker, he is also a rule follower. He doesn't like when his classmates break the rules. This is how I knew he was also watching and paying attention. While Karson and his brother Kade have their own distinct personalities, they do have something in common, they both are goal driven. When we would buy Karson a game, within a couple of days, sometimes hours, he would have the game beat. Karson began Tao Kwon Do at the age of six. I was always impressed with all the forms that they had to learn to get to the next colored belt. Karson set a goal to become a black belt and accomplished that goal several years later.

Karson set a goal to start his own YouTube channel at the age of thirteen. He did all the research and set up all the production for the channel on his own. We were very impressed with the content. He did an amazing job. Recently, he started writing and has completed his first book titled, Powerless. This is quite impressive for a sophomore in high school. He has already begun writing Volume two of Powerless, along with another book in the works. My relationship with my youngest son has impacted me in so many wonderful ways, but mostly, I have learned to love unconditionally, to not judge someone before you get all the facts, and maybe walk in their shoes. Through Karson, I've learned that being kind is cool and one liners are important in conversation. I love you, Karson, and I know that you will achieve the dreams you set for yourself.

Mia Grace

Mia is a gift from above, and her name means "my blessing". Karson and Kade are the perfect big brothers to her because they will do anything for her, and she knows this. She is the typical youngest sibling and gets her way a lot, but rarely do the boys complain. Since Karson and Mia are only seventeen months apart, it was a blessing that Karson was such an easy toddler which allowed us to spend the time we needed taking care of a newborn when he himself was still a baby. Kade was great with Karson as well, playing with him and keeping him occupied.

The first and only girl after the two boys was so different but also amazing. Our laundry became a lot pinker and our hearts even fuller when Mia was born. Mia and Karson got along great and played so well together. Even when they were little, Karson would allow Mia to get her way as the little sister. Throughout their pre-K and elementary school years, Kade was in football, Karson was in Taekwondo and Mia was in ballet. It was difficult but rewarding. How Kandice did all of this while I was coaching, I still do not know. I would meet her at either dance practice, the football field, or the dojo. One of us would take the other kids home and get dinner ready. It was difficult, but we communicated and worked it out. I can honestly say that I miss those days of running the kids all around town. I am not sure about Kandice since she is the one that did most of the ubering.

When Mia was three, she was so ready to start school that she would get upset when her brothers had homework and she didn't. She liked things a certain way and we knew she would like the structure that school offered. She was blessed with two older brothers who have set great examples of being respectful and well-mannered students. Her desire to go to school and follow in her brothers' footsteps let me know that again, she was watching. One memory that stands out from when Mia was little is when she performed at The Woodlands Pavillion with her ballet group to a song called "In her Father's Shoes." During the dance, the girls stepped in their dad's shoes and danced. I would have given her the keys to my car after that.

In addition to being a talented dancer, Mia is very artistically and musically talented. Her drawings are amazing and detailed. She works very hard for the band at Klein Collins where she plays the French Horn. Mia has always been a person that knows what she wants and will stand up to make her own path. She is a hard worker and has excelled in school, in various activities, and in creative outlets such as art and music. My relationship with my daughter has impacted me in endless ways. I have learned about the strength we have inside ourselves and that she will surely be able to take care of herself through any situation. She has seen her Mom, her Maui. and her Grandma handle situations with class and laughter. She will be able to carry this into her own life. I love you, Mia, and I know that whatever you strive to do in life, you will make it happen.

Kandice, Kade, Karson and Mia are my why. They are the reason that I remain consistent, and they are the reason I get up and grind daily. I want the most important people in my life to know that I cherish them. I will always be available and there to support them. They influence me to be the best husband and father that I can be.

## ABOUT THE AUTHOR:

Social Media:
**LI** @MannyTrujillo
**Email** mankantrujillo@att.net

Manny Trujillo is a second generation teacher/coach who just completed his twenty-fourth year in education. He was born and raised in Hearne, Texas, where he graduated from Hearne High School. He later received his bachelor degree in kinesiology and education from Sam Houston State University. His wife, Kandice, is also an educator with twenty seven years of teaching experience. His oldest son, Kade, is a junior, majoring in industrial distribution at Texas A&M University. His youngest son, Karson, is a sophomore at Klein Collins High School and his only daughter, Mia, is a freshman at Klein Collins High School.

# HANGOVER
**Megan Marie Randall**

"Life is simple. Everything happens for you, not to you. Everything happens at exactly the right moment, neither too soon nor too late. You don't have to like it…it's just easier if you do."
-Byron Katie

I want to kindly start by stating, that if you have made it to this point, I need you to stand up and walk to your bathroom mirror. Look at that intelligent person staring back at you and tell them, "I am so proud of you! You are reading, you are growing and you are succeeding! I love YOU so much!"

Did you do it yet? If not, this is your permission to take a quick timeout, stop, and go do that before you continue reading.

How do you feel? A little empowered perhaps? Maybe a little more confident and influenced? Good! You should be! If you're not, stop right now and go back to the mirror. Really take your time to reflect and dig deep as you look back at that mirror.

Why am I asking you to do this you ask? Because I want, and feel the need, to share a story about this girl I know. I love her dearly and have been influenced by her for many years. Her vulnerability, passion to connect and serve, love for others, and her strength to keep moving forward has impacted me every day in a different way. Maybe it will for you too!

As we were having coffee one morning, she opened her heart and started acknowledging her past with me. She shared with me how she learned to tie her shoes and how it caused her to have a life hangover.

She was three years old. She was wearing an oversized woolly, knit lavender sweater with white smiley faces all over it. She had on blue jeans and her hair was in a messy side ponytail with untied shoelaces that were tucked in the sides of her shoes.

Her dad at that time, yelled from the kitchen, "Come on, let's go."

She jumped up curiously, leaving the television on while it continued to play 'The Price is Right'. As she walked into the front room, he said sternly, "Sit down and tie your shoes."

She worriedly looked up at him and timidly responded, "I don't know how."

He again told her to sit down, as his body directed toward the wooden rocker chair in the front room. She propped herself up and looked at him in wonder and then down to her left shoe. As he finished tying her left shoelaces expecting her to watch and learn quickly, he told her, "Now tie the right one".

She curiously leaned forward, grabbed her right two laces, one in each hand, slowly crossed them to make a big 'X' and she suddenly felt lost. She said softly, "I forget."

The very next moment she felt a pain strike her face so alarming that her body plunged into the arm of the wooden rocker. Tears flooded her eyes as she came to realize the pain, and fear began to diffuse within her entire body.

"I don't have time for this, now hurry the hell up and tie your shoe!" He yelled.

As she heard the cheering in the background from the television still playing, she looked at him frightfully and cried, "I don't know how, where's papa?!"

As his impatience and frustration grew, he was in a hurry to leave and didn't want to hear her cry, so he again raised his hand up and slapped her across her face a second time. She was panic-stricken and shaking but began to see that she had to obey him because there was no other way out. She was stuck and had to tie her shoe.

She reached down, grabbed the untied right laces, made the big 'X' again but thought harder to remember through her sobs. She tucked one under the other in the big hole and pulled them together. She froze in fear and started to cry harder. She forgot what was next again and knew that she would be hurt.

His anger boiled with impatience as he looked at her and aggressively stated, "Are you really that stupid?" He grabbed her arm tightly, squeezed with force and pulled her towards him. He proceeded to tell her, "I'm showing you one last damn time and if you don't do it, you're not seeing your grandparents at all!" Then shoved her back into the chair.

At that moment she was completely scared and terrified. Her heart was racing, her breathing was intense, and her throat was tight. Her grandparents were her everything and her safety. She was still hurting from the pain in her arm from the squeeze and fearful of upsetting him again. She desperately wanted to tie her shoe just so he would be happy, and she could run away and hide somewhere, somehow.

Unfortunately, this event went on for another thirty minutes, but to her felt like an eternity. She finally tied her shoe twice in a row. Instead of hugging or nurturing her, he told her to hurry up and go shut the television off. She ran into the living room, saw the winner of 'The Price is Right' and wished her grandpa was there with her. That was a time they shared together with laughs and smiles while watching. She headed out to the car, jumped in the front seat and cried herself into a deep sleep.

She continued to reflect on this moment with me as I cried with her. This was a memory she had purposely tried to avoid, but deep down it was a moment in time she could never forget. It ended up affecting her in many ways of her life journey that she never knew until just a few years ago.

For years, she was frightened to fail at anything or even upset someone she cared about. It was as if her body couldn't forget the outcome of that experience. It subconsciously stuck with her and her internal development. Whether it was understanding something as simple as numbers, her work pay with her boss, or if she disappointed a man she was dating. Even if it was just a simple disagreement with her taste in music. She even panicked internally if she was ever late for a new friend, client, or co-worker. Deep down panic would set in, tears crept up into her tear ducts, and her heart would begin to beat rapidly, all out of control. All because of that moment she experienced learning on how to tie her shoes.

Through the years, she utilized many strategies, thinking that by doing these strategies they would fulfill her and many others that entered into her life. From being a high achiever, a people pleaser, a control freak, an approval seeker, comedian and even miss busy bee.

If she ever had a moment where she assumed or thought she wasn't enough, not doing something right, was slow, annoying, or disappointing someone, she would subconsciously utilize these strategies. By accomplishing a goal, maybe she could make up for the fact that she was slow in other areas or even attain the attention and love from others. If she really liked a guy, she would turn into a chameleon. She thought if she liked everything he liked, he would want her more or be more attracted to her. If she could control and put together these big parties for others or make jokes when she met someone new who was out of her league, perhaps more of them would approve of her and want to be her friend. She would also make herself busy with work, so she would receive approval from others and avoid her emotions. There was no time to be a victim or be upset. That was not attractive or appealing. She even became overly affectionate and nurturing in her relationships thinking that that would cause someone to love her back. She acted out like this for many years, not knowing it wasn't the correct way to gain true connection. All she ever wanted and knew was that she wanted to feel loved and accepted by others.

The 'she' I am referring to you in this story, is me.

I finally experienced a breakthrough within myself. After seeing pictures of me jumping out of a plane for my best friend, the thought that crossed my mind was, 'If I can jump out of a plane and possibly kill myself for him just to see his smile on his birthday, why can't I do that for myself and my own true happiness?' After acknowledging and realizing that none of these strategies were working towards my happiness, I decided I needed to change things up. Yes, people were coming into my life, but none were sticking and staying. I was always getting that feeling of waiting for the other shoe to drop, as if I couldn't get too happy, because something was going to happen to me. I would wonder around my house for hours on some days thinking, "Why? What am I doing wrong? Why am I not fulfilled or happy, even on days that I am alone?"

I have become this successful, beautiful, and loving woman that I am so incredibly proud of and influenced by. I discontinued several old strategies and replaced them with things that fascinated me or that I loved. Things such as reading, writing, a podcast, and connecting deeper with people when I meet them, just to name a few. During this breakthrough, I learned from other mentors. People like my therapist. Other amazing authors, Christine Hassler, and Podcaster Jay Shetty. When these 'Life Hangovers' happen, I have different outfits I can wear so my hangover doesn't last as long as it has before. I can still have fun living in the moment while learning!

When something doesn't work out as you planned change your outfit by dressing as a horseback rider. Let me explain. As a horseback rider, you need to 'whoa yourself', just as a rider would 'whoa' their horse to slow down when pacing too quickly or needing to stop for a breather. When you are in a moment of agitation, confusion, self-doubt, anger, fear or even worry, 'whoa' yourself. Think back to when you felt like this for the very first time. More than likely, you were little. You may have felt like you failed and weren't enough. It caused you to feel and develop these emotions at that moment in time. Once you acknowledge that moment you now get to change your clothes and become…a surfer.

As a surfer you need to ride out that wave of emotion. Surfers don't see an incredible wave and jump off to go swim. They gather up their courage, jump up on the board, face that wave and ride it to the very end. That's how we have to reflect and treat this memory. Acknowledge when it started. Be courageous and reflect on it. Truly ride out that entire emotion until it's out of your system. Too many times we try to avoid the feeling by staying busy with work or run away from the feeling by avoiding it, which isn't the right way to truly get better. Don't be scared, remember to be successful you have do the things you don't want to do in order to be successful (thanks Mr.Rohn). Keep your head up and ride that wave. You may cry. You can write. You can talk about it with that parent. Whatever it takes, just ride out that wave and quit avoiding it!

Once you've accomplished that wave, you guessed it, wardrobe change! Put on that lab coat and let's endure being a scientist! Our past strategies haven't worked since we are still feeling that lack of fulfillment. By strategies, I am referring to those previous methods I mentioned that I was doing subconsciously: high achiever, people pleasing, miss busy etc. Those were methods I thought would work, just like a hypothesis. Once I realized they didn't work, I put it under a mental microscope and acknowledged where it began. I reflected on what I had done and tried. Now it's time to change few ingredients or try something new. Which is fine because not every hypothesis is successful! They are constantly changing. Now please note, even if you found that great love, dream job, finally have that loving family, or spectacular body, you never want to think, "Great, I've finally arrived, that's all folks!"

We never arrive because with the new chapter comes new tests. As I mentioned, we may need to change the hypothesis a little with these new tests. If you stay in that mindset that you've arrived and are finished, then depression can easily start to linger in your direction. Stay curious, more so within yourself and be open minded to change. Change is hard, but possible, and even quite fun along the way!

Ready for your last outfit? Great! Let's change and become a seeker. Everyone deep down should always try daily to dig deeper within themselves and their god, higher power or whatever that may be for you. This is so crucial for you because it's an opportunity for you to find out what your current superpowers are, which is what fascinates you. Also, to realize what core values you would like to incorporate. By recognizing these two major elements of your life you will become inspired to take more action and come out with results that lead to your true inner fulfillment. You will finally experience the richness of your own self love and happiness along the way!

I'm sharing this with you in a summarized chapter. I wanted to give you insight of just one of my hangovers I discovered. I wanted to share what I learned to be more compassionate and graceful within myself.

It is ok to love and influence yourself! That's not conceited. That's self-confidence! You must learn and understand deep down that that self-love is necessary to truly love and connect with others. Being inspired within yourself is such a beautiful and fulfilling experience. As I told you in the very beginning of this chapter, go back and look in that mirror. Take a deep hard look at that beautiful and loving soul. You need to be proud of them and congratulate them for not just surviving the day, but for thriving every single day!

What outfit will you change into today? I would love to see and hear all about it, so don't be scared to share your success story with me or any others. You may just influence someone else along the way without even knowing about it!

Xoxo,
Megan Marie

## ABOUT THE AUTHOR:

Social Media:
**IG** @BluEyezz0124
**Website** MeganMarieEntity.com
**Email** MM@MeganMarieEntity.com

Megan Marie is the CEO of Megan Marie Entity providing travel tips on her blog, weight loss secrets, her podcast 'The Megan Marie Show' and affiliate marketing with other influential entrepreneurs. All of which are accessible on her website: MeganMarieEntity.com She has been a record-breaking insurance agent for the last eleven years representing the same company. She graduated from Indiana State University with a Bachelors in Communications and Journalism. She is also a Best-Selling Author thanks to the last edition of The Impact of Influence vol.5.

She loves reading, writing, traveling to new places, (especially beaches), her puppy Drake, music, and quality conversations. She is always interested in learning new things that bring value into her life. Her purpose and passion in life are serving others and building a crescendo of love and happiness wherever it takes her. She is an Aquarius who is always growing, always learning and always ready for an adrenaline rush!

# FREE TO FAIL: THE TENETS OF FINDING SUCCESS THROUGH FAILURES.
**Olaolu Ogunyemi**

It was another hot, humid day in Quantico, Virginia, July 2011. My platoon at the United States Marine Corps Officer Candidates School (OCS) was training on the obstacle course (o-course). Although I grew up playing sports, I had never experienced the physical exertion associated with traversing an o-course. It seemed daunting at first–especially when we had to balance on the parallel logs. However, my nervousness waned with each of the countless repetitions we completed.

We focused on the final obstacle on this particular day–the twenty-foot rope climb. Ironically, the rope climb is arguably one of the easiest obstacles…if you have the proper technique. Of course, I did not have the proper technique! I relied mainly on my upper body strength to grind through this final obstacle. Regardless, I made it to the top, slapped the log, and triumphantly screamed, "Candidate Ogunyemi, Bravo Company, Second Platoon!"

My platoon sergeant was furious when I came down. "Ogunyemi," he barked, "one day, you're going to FAIL!"

It seemed like the word "fail" was one of his favorite words to yell, and he was literally the loudest man I have ever met (and that includes my time as a Series and Company Commander at the

Marine Corps Recruit Depot San Diego). Something was different this time. For starters, he said my actual name instead of whatever else he could think to call me that started with an "o" like "origami." No, something was off.

## My failures at OCS

I started a gruesome physical training routine as soon as I decided to join the Marine Corps in 2010. I was convinced that I would conquer any physical challenge the Marine Corps would throw my way! Admittedly, I knew absolutely nothing about the Marine Corps other than the cool things I saw in movies, the news, and commercials. This was evident because–little known fact–I had so many academic failures while at OCS that I was forced to explain what I would do to improve at a company retention board! Thankfully, the company commander decided to retain me, and I continued to pursue my dreams of becoming a U.S. Marine.

Contextually, it's easy to understand why my platoon sergeant was infuriated by my inability or unwillingness to master the rope climb technique. My opposing perspective was that I accomplished the mission, so his frustration was unjustified! Either way, I felt vindicated a few weeks later when I completed the graded o-course and graduated in August 2011. That vindication "high" lasted until I arrived at The Basic School where we had to complete two consecutive intervals of the o-course for time.

## The double o-course

I finished the first interval much quicker and easier than I expected! Seeing my peers zip through the course must've given me the confidence I needed to perform well myself. I started the second interval winded but not exhausted. My strategy was to keep it steady as I built upon the momentum gained by my desire to beat the lieutenant navigating the parallel course. I gained a slight advantage as I was able to bound over the final logs more easily than my counterpart. Then came my final obstacle which would soon establish itself as my arch nemesis–the rope.

I approached the rope as I did numerous times before to begin my climb. I jumped as high as I could before grabbing the rope to lessen the distance I'd have to climb. Then, I used the "J hook" method to secure myself to the rope using my feet. Lastly, I began climbing using mainly my upper body strength while using my feet to stop myself from sliding back down. The extreme exhaustion turned this rather routine event into a grueling escapade.

"You're almost done!" I told myself. It wasn't long before I felt my shoulder muscles trembling. Uh oh. I was only halfway through my climb! "Just keep pushing!" I thought to myself. I grinded through about another six feet and stopped. My shoulders had completely locked up and I couldn't climb any further! I audibly told myself every motivational cliché I could think of, but my muscles were done. I knew I would soon lose my grip and fall sixteen feet to the ground if I didn't climb down.

After several more unsuccessful (and embarrassing) attempts, I finally gave up–tired, defeated, and sore. I could hear my loud-mouth platoon sergeant's voice echoing in my head; "You failed!"

### What did this failure (and others like it) teach me?

This is just one of the many failures I've had in life. Some, like this one, were public which greatly contributed to the embarrassment and proverbial whiplash I received as a result. What if I told you I learned something from these failures? Would you believe me if I told you that these failures have been crucial to my success? Would you call me crazy if I shared that I welcome failure now? That's right! I have freed myself to succeed through my failures, and I want you to do the same! With that in mind, I will share my advice on how to do just that.

## Tenet 1: Failure is rarely fun.

I want to begin by telling you something you already know: failure is rarely fun. Seriously! You think I liked people seeing me struggle on that rope? I was one of the few out of over two hundred people who didn't successfully complete the double o-course. All the training, preparation, three-a-day workouts, and motivational messages seemed for naught as I feverishly struggled on that rope like a fish hopelessly trying to free itself from a line. I'm not exaggerating when I say it was one of the most embarrassing moments of my life.

In that moment, I felt hopeless and desperate. The confidence I built as a result of many years of playing sports and exercising was instantly zapped from my body. This obstacle had proven to be insurmountable.

Before I could use this failure to influence my success, I had to acknowledge and absorb the impact it had on my emotions. Admittedly, this was a challenge for me because my skewed perspective of masculinity and "toughness" stifled my ability to explore these thoughts, feelings, and emotions. Contrarily, I've learned over the years that this is the first–and arguably the most important–step to experience freedom through failure and achieve success. Acknowledge and validate your feelings, develop an action plan to restore your mental and spiritual health, and begin the healing process.

*Try this:

On my blog (https://www.parent-child-connect.com/blog), I described how we can practice moving from our reactive emotions to establishing a "healing" action plan using a concept called the "5 why's." This exercise will help you identify and address the root cause of your emotions by developing a "countermeasure." The exercise is simple: you state the emotion you're feeling, then ask "why" five times. Here's a quick example! (Yes, it's a basketball reference.):

I am sad.

Why? (One)

I am embarrassed that someone blocked my game-winning layup.

Why? (Two)

I was having such a great game.

Why? (Three)

I practiced extremely hard to prepare for this game.

Why? (Four)

This was a really big game.

Why? (Five)

This was my final opportunity to play in front of my family and friends before the season ended.

Countermeasure: I will connect with my family and friends, discuss my feelings when I feel comfortable, and celebrate a great game and fulfilling season.

## Tenet 2: Failure is not fatal.

As I stood there preparing to plead my case to my company commander at OCS, I was nervous, embarrassed, and lost. How could someone who maintained above a 3.5 grade point average his entire life be on a retention board at OCS for academic failures? Regardless of my thoughts and emotions, I had to square myself away and plead my case with confidence. I was determined that my failures would not kill my dream to become a U.S. Marine. They didn't!

In fact, my failures as a candidate at OCS helped me to connect with and encourage another candidate who was on the same board as me. My failures also helped me become more empathetic towards others, and I've had the pleasure of mentoring several phenomenal leaders who had to overcome challenges during entry-level training and in the early years of their careers.

My reluctance to equate my failures to "the end" has made me more resilient and broadened my perspective to accept failure as inevitable while rejecting the notion that failure should always be associated with a negative connotation. Failure is not the end of our dreams and ambitions; it is the portal to limitless potential and achievements.

*Try this:
1. Write down a recent failure you encountered that felt like it killed your dream.
2. Google search exactly what you just wrote down. Did you find similar stories?
3. How did the examples you found overcome this adversity?
4. What ideas from this research can you use to create your own "portal to limitless potential and achievements?"
5. Who can help you along the way?

**Tenet 3: Use "failure" as a verb...not a noun.**

Trust me, this is not going to be a revolutionary tenet. In fact, you probably learned this around second or third grade, but I am stating the obvious to drive a point home. A verb–specifically an "action verb" in this context–describes something that the noun did. For example, consider the following sentence: "Billy drove the car." "Billy" is the subject or "noun" in the sentence. "Drove" is the "verb" that describes what Billy did.

WAIT!...Hear me out before you close the book. There's a reason I'm making this elementary observation.

My point is simple: many of us forget this elemental truth once we rack up a few failures. We say things like, "maybe this just isn't meant to be" before we ultimately give up on our dreams. The momentum seems to have shifted, our confidence is shot, and we no longer have the energy we once had. We find ourselves flopping at the bottom of the proverbial rope, desperate to make it to the top. Let this be your encouragement and reminder.: No matter how many times you've failed (verb), your failures do not determine your identity (noun).

YOU get to choose your identity and destiny! Don't let anyone tell you otherwise.

## Tenet 4: Shift your perspective to see opportunities instead of obstacles.

I'm sure some of you are wondering if I ever successfully climbed the rope and completed the double o-course. Well, the answer is, "YES!"...But it wasn't easy! I worked on my full body strength and muscle endurance and spent countless hours practicing the technique while learning from others. Frankly, I considered giving up as the adrenaline rush I received from being embarrassed started to dwindle over time. I'm a firm believer that results will always be inconsistent if they are driven by emotion. I needed to identify and address the true problem.

### The true problem.

The problem was I had lost sight of my ultimate goal–which was to graduate from The Basic School. Once I recalibrated my mind to focus on my goal, I realized the rope wasn't truly an obstacle; it was the means to an end. I'll explain it like this.:

Oxford Languages defines "obstacle" as, "a thing that blocks one's way or prevents or hinders progress." Regardless of how much some choose to deny it, human nature is to always follow the path of least resistance. Therefore, to psychologically accept the rope (or any other obstacle) as a blockade or hindrance is to create an insurmountable barrier between myself and my goal. Contrarily, I began to view the rope as an "opportunity" which Oxford Languages defines as, "a time or set of circumstances that makes it possible to do something." I submit that we all should adopt this philosophy!

We tend to view life as a series of mountains and valleys, ups and downs, or an "obstacle course." Be that as it may, I'm challenging you to view life as an opportunity course! Getting passed for promotion may be your opportunity to seek employment elsewhere. Getting rejected may be your opportunity to refine your sales pitch. Failing a test may be your opportunity to make a new friend and study partner. Struggling to climb a rope may be your opportunity to build your strength and endurance. You get my point?

We are no longer traversing an obstacle course–running from one discouraging barrier into another. We are growing stronger as we bound from opportunity to opportunity!

## Tenet 5: Success begins with failure.

I love observing babies and toddlers as they interact with the world around them. They just wander around without a care in the world! Their nonchalant and naive attitude makes them a special bunch that many of us have grown to be proud of. One of the proudest moments is the toddler's first steps!

We record, cheer, cry, laugh, celebrate, and just make a huge deal out of it. Here's the interesting thing about it: most toddlers fail to walk hundreds of times! Have you ever thought about that? The overall goal is for them to walk like adult human beings. Why do we get so excited when they wobble in the most uncoordinated manner possible for about two steps before they fall?

Good parents and caregivers encourage and cheer for their toddler as they progress towards their ultimate goal. We determine that the two uncoordinated steps are more important than the hundreds of failed attempts because we believe that continued practice will produce the desired results. The problem is we forget this philosophical truth somewhere along the line.

As time progresses, we lose patience with failure as it doesn't present the immediate results we are looking for. I challenge you to embrace the "wobbly toddler" faith again as you focus on your progress instead of your failures.

## Tenet 6: Failing is freeing, so feel free to fail!

I know this entire chapter is countercultural and it may make you uncomfortable, but trust me; these tenets work! Ever since I shifted my perspective on failure, I have felt an unexplainable freedom. Additionally, I was able to redirect the energy I spent sulking in my failures towards progressing towards my ultimate goal which is to live out my purpose. I learned to loosen the reins I thought I had on life to live a more enjoyable and healthy life.

I will leave you with this: Control what you can control. Influence what you can influence. Let everything else go. Your success in life and ability to live out your purpose is predicated on your willingness to shift your perspective on failure. Feel free to fail and begin your journey towards success today!

# ABOUT THE AUTHOR:

Social Media:
**LI** Olaolu Ogunyemi
**Website** https://parent-child-connect.com
**Email** parentchildconnectemail@gmail.com

Olaolu Ogunyemi is a loving husband, father, teen mentor, and U.S. Marine Officer with a deep passion for working with children fueled by an unending supply of energy and imagination! Since he was young, Olaolu has been nicknamed the "life of the party" because he pours his exuberant personality into everything he does. As the fifth of six children, he became intimately familiar with the bond forged during quality story time; thus, Olaolu was inspired to start writing children's stories to help create loving and memorable family moments. He is the author of the Amazon best-selling children's book, "Crow From the Shadow," "Horace the Horsefly," and "Billy Dipper's Time to Shine."

Olaolu writes and speaks in a simple, easily understandable language and with an entertaining style that keeps families and listeners hooked while learning vital lessons about virtues and sparking a continuing conversation.

Olaolu is a frequent traveler and in his free time, he enjoys playing music, exercising, writing, and spending time with his family.

## THE BUTTERFLY EFFECT
**Victor Pisano**

""Believe that life is worth living and your belief will help create the fact."
- William James

The "Butterfly Effect" is a term used to describe the idea that small actions or events can have significant and far-reaching consequences. It is based on the idea that even a seemingly small and insignificant event or action can potentially have a significant impact on the future, similar to how the flapping of a butterfly's wings in one part of the world can potentially lead to a tornado in another part of the world.

The concept was first introduced by meteorologist Edward Lorenz in the 1960s, who observed that small differences in the initial conditions of a weather system could result in significantly different weather patterns over time. For example, the presence or absence of a single cloud in the sky could potentially lead to very different weather patterns in the future.

In the same way that small actions or events can have significant consequences in the physical world, it is also possible for small acts of positivity to have a significant and far-reaching impact on the world and those around us. This is because the way we think, feel, and behave can affect not only our own lives, but also the lives of those around us. When we act with positivity, we can inspire others to do the same, and this can create a ripple effect of positivity that spreads throughout our communities and beyond. For example, a simple act of kindness such as holding the door open for someone or offering a helping hand to a friend in need may seem small, but it can have a big impact on the person receiving the kindness. It may inspire them to pay it forward, leading to a chain reaction of positive influence.

There are many ways that we can create positivity in our lives and in the world around us. Some simple ways to do this include:
- Practice gratitude and focus on the positive things in your life.
- Perform acts of kindness, such as volunteering, helping a neighbor, or donating to a charity.
- Spread positivity by sharing uplifting messages or content online or with those around you.
- Practice mindfulness and focus on the present moment, rather than dwelling on negative thoughts or events from the past.
- Surround yourself with positive, supportive people and avoid negativity when possible.

By taking small steps to cultivate positivity in our own lives and in the world around us, we can potentially create a butterfly effect of positivity that spreads far and wide. When I think of "influence," and privilege, I must earn the trust of others I work with through my character and leadership development programs. The butterfly effect is my way of simplifying the intent on why I want to elicit the greatness out of each person.

Influence is a powerful force that can shape the way we think, feel, and behave. It can come from many sources, including friends, family, media, and even strangers. The ability to influence others can be a valuable skill, whether you're a leader, a parent, or simply trying to persuade someone to see things your way.

One of the most common ways that people exert influence is through social proof. This is the idea that we tend to look to others for cues on how to behave. For example, if you see a group of people laughing at a joke, you're more likely to find the joke funny too. Similarly, if you see a group of people wearing a particular style of clothing, you might be more likely to adopt that style yourself.

Another way that people influence others is through charisma and charm. Some people seem to have an almost magnetic quality that draws others to them. They have the ability to persuade and inspire others through their words and actions. Charismatic leaders, for example, can inspire their followers to achieve great things.

Influence can also be exercised through authority. People are more likely to follow the orders of someone they perceive as an authority figure, whether it's a boss, a teacher, or a police officer. Authority figures can use their position to influence others through rewards and punishments. In addition to these more overt forms of influence, there are also subtle ways that people can influence others. For example, someone might use emotional manipulation to try and get what they want. They might use guilt, shame, or fear to try and persuade someone to do something they want.

Overall, the power of influence is undeniable. It can be used for good or for ill. It's important to be aware of the ways that it can shape our thoughts and actions. By understanding the various ways that influence can be exercised, we can better protect ourselves from being swayed by others and make more informed decisions for ourselves.

Social influence is also a powerful force. We are constantly influenced by the actions and behaviors of those around us, whether it's through peer pressure or the desire to fit in with a particular group. Therefore, companies often try to create a sense of community around their products or services - they know that people are more likely to buy into something if they feel like they are part of a group.

Influence can also come from within. Our own thoughts and beliefs can influence our actions and decisions. This is why it's important to be mindful of the things we allow ourselves to be exposed to, as they can shape our beliefs and ultimately influence our behavior. The power of influence is vast and far-reaching. It can come from a variety of sources and can shape our thoughts, behaviors, and decisions in profound ways. By being mindful of the sources of influence in our lives, we can make more informed and conscious decisions.

The power of positive influence is an often overlooked but incredibly important aspect of human interactions. It has the ability to transform not only our own lives, but also the lives of those around us. Positive influence can be described as the ability to inspire and motivate others to be their best selves, to think positively, and to act in ways that are beneficial for themselves and those around them. It can come from many different sources, including friends, family, teachers, mentors, and role models.

One of the most powerful ways in which positive influence can have an impact is through the spread of positive attitudes and behaviors. When we are around people who are optimistic, supportive, and encouraging, we are more likely to adopt these same attitudes and behaviors ourselves. This can have a ripple effect, as we then go on to influence others in the same way. This can create a virtuous cycle of positivity that has the potential to spread throughout entire communities and even beyond. Positive influence can also have a powerful impact on our own personal development. When we are surrounded by people who inspire us to be better, we are more likely to set and achieve higher goals for ourselves. This can lead to increased confidence, self-esteem, and a greater sense of purpose and fulfillment in life.

One key way in which positive influence can be exercised is through the power of role modeling. When we see someone who we admire and respect doing something that we aspire to do ourselves, it can be incredibly motivating. For example, if we see a successful entrepreneur who is hardworking, innovative, and passionate about their work, we may be inspired to pursue our own entrepreneurial dreams. Similarly, if we see someone who is kind, compassionate, and selfless, we may be more likely to strive to be the same way ourselves.

Another way in which positive influence can be exercised is through the power of encouragement and support. When we receive encouragement and support from those around us, we are more likely to believe in ourselves and to feel capable of achieving our goals. This can be especially powerful for people who are struggling with self-doubt or who may be facing challenges in their lives.

Positive influence can also have a profound impact on our relationships with others. When we are surrounded by people who are positive and supportive, we are more likely to form strong and lasting relationships with them. This can create a sense of belonging and community that can be incredibly nourishing and fulfilling. There are those people in our lives that have always provided positivity and have served as a moral compass in our journey. I cherish those relationships, and in time, these people have become my mentors. Their example elicits the greatness out of me that I never knew I had. It is a result of these experiences that I look at being an influence on others as privilege – not an obligation – to pay it forward.

There are many ways in which we can exercise positive influence in our own lives and in the lives of those around us. Some examples might include:

- Being a good listener: By actively listening to others and truly hearing what they have to say, we can show them that we care and that we are there for them. This can be incredibly powerful in building trust and strengthening relationships.
- Practicing kindness: By being kind and compassionate towards others, we can inspire them to be the same way. This can be as simple as offering a smile or a kind word, or as significant as volunteering our time or resources to help those in need.

- Being a good role model: By living our lives in a way that is authentic, honest, and true to our values, we can inspire others to do the same. This can be especially powerful for young people who may be looking for guidance and direction.
- Offering encouragement and support: By offering encouragement and support to those around us, we can help them to feel more confident and capable of achieving their goals. This can be as simple as offering a word of encouragement or as significant as providing practical support and resources.
- Leading by example: By setting a good example in our own lives, we can inspire others to follow suit.
- Develop strong communication skills: Being able to communicate effectively and clearly is key to being able to influence others. This includes being able to listen actively, speak persuasively, and manage conflicts effectively.
- Be a good role model: Leading by example is a powerful way to influence others. By consistently demonstrating positive behavior and attitudes, you can inspire and motivate those around you to follow suit.
- Be confident and authentic: Confidence and authenticity are attractive qualities that can help you gain the respect and trust of others. Be genuine and true to yourself, and others will be more likely to follow your lead.
- Foster positive relationships: Building strong, positive relationships with others is essential to being able to influence them. Take the time to get to know people and build trust and rapport with them.
- Have a clear vision and plan: People are more likely to follow those who have a clear vision and a plan for achieving it. Define your goals and ideas clearly and communicate them effectively to others.

- Practice empathy and compassion: Showing empathy and compassion towards others can help you build strong connections with them and inspire them to follow your lead.
- Be a continuous learner: Stay current on developments in your field and seek out new knowledge and skills. This will not only help you stay relevant, but also demonstrate to others that you are committed to personal and professional growth.

It is widely recognized that positive influence can have a powerful impact on individuals, groups, and society as a whole. When we engage in positive behaviors and attitudes, we not only improve our own well-being and sense of happiness, but we also have the ability to inspire and motivate those around us to do the same. This can create a ripple effect of positivity that can lead to significant and lasting change in the world.

In addition to the emotional and psychological benefits of positive influence, research has also shown that it can have tangible, practical benefits as well. For example, studies have found that individuals who engage in positive thinking and behavior tend to be more successful in their personal and professional lives, and that organizations with a positive culture tend to be more innovative and productive.

Overall, the power of positive influence is undeniable and has the potential to bring about significant and lasting change in the world. Whether through our own actions or by inspiring others to be their best selves, we all have the ability to make a positive impact on those around us. It's all about making an impact, one that leaves an ever-lasting impression of positivity. It takes a committed effort toward reframing the narrative and wanting to be a difference maker.

There are many ways that you can make a positive impact in the world, no matter who you are or what your circumstances may be. Here are a few ideas:

- Volunteer your time and talents to help others. There are many organizations that rely on volunteers to carry out their important work. Whether you prefer to work with children, animals, the environment, or any other cause, there is likely a volunteer opportunity that aligns with your interests and values.
- Support organizations and causes that are important to you. Donating money or resources to organizations that are making a positive impact can be a powerful way to support their work and make a difference in the world.
- Be a positive influence in your own community. Even small acts of kindness and generosity can make a big difference in the lives of those around you. Whether it's helping a neighbor in need, volunteering at a local school, or simply being a good friend, there are many ways to make a positive impact in your own community.

Remember, the key is to find a way to make a difference that feels meaningful and fulfilling to you. With determination and a commitment to making a positive impact, you can make a difference in the world.

Go be a butterfly today!

Do great things today and make a difference.

Humbled to lead,
Victor Pisano

# ABOUT THE AUTHOR:

Social Media:
**IG** @charge_up_today
**Website** www.chargeuptoday.com
**Email** chargeup@satx.rr.com

Victor Pisano has inspired executives, entrepreneurs, leaders, high school and college student-athletes across the country with his leadership platform, Charge Up. At the core of its foundation is that leadership is both a gift and a privilege, and we must pay it forward and elicit the greatness in others to make a positive impact. To inspire and empower people who are willing to invest in their goals and push past the barriers so that they can discover their passion, find their purpose, and have the courage to act with integrity as they pursue their path to fulfillment. Speaking for over twenty years, he is also certified as a speaker and trainer through the John Maxwell Academy, Jon Gordon's "Power of a Positive Leader," and the Third Rivers, "Leading with Values" program. He has also collaborated on four Amazon Best-Selling Books, "The Impact of Influence - Volume One", "The Impact of Influence – Volume Two", and "The Impact of Influence – Volume Five," and "Concrete Connections."

Visit him at www.chargeuptoday.com

# ABOUT THE LEAD AUTHOR

Chip Baker is a fourth-generation educator. He has been a teacher and coach for over twenty-two years. He is a multiple-time best-selling author, YouTuber, podcaster, motivational speaker, and life coach.

Chip Baker is the creator of the YouTube channel and podcast *Chip Baker—The Success Chronicles*, where he interviews people from all walks of life and shares their stories for positive inspiration and motivation.

Live. Learn. Serve. Inspire. Go get it!

**Email:** chipbakertsc@gmail.com
**Online Store:**
http://chip-baker-the-success-chronicles.square.site/
**Facebook Page:**
https://www.facebook.com/TSCChipBaker
**Instagram:** @chipbakertsc
**LinkedIn:**
https://www.linkedin.com/in/chipbakerthesuccesschronicles/
**Twitter:** @chipbaker19

*Chip Baker—The Success Chronicles*
**YouTube:** youtube.com/c/ChipBakerTheSuccessChronicles
**Podcast:** https://anchor.fm/chip-baker

**Other Books:**
*Growing Through Your Go Through*
*Effective Conversation to Ignite Relationships*
*Suited for Success, Vol. 2*
*The Formula Chart for Life*
*The Impact of Influence Vol. 1,2, 3, 4, & 5*
*R.O.C.K. Solid*
*Stay on the Right Path*
*Black Men Love*
*The Winning Mindset*
*Concrete Connections*

# PICK UP THESE OTHER TITLES BY CHIP BAKER

 GROWING THROUGH YOUR GO THROUGH

 EFFECTIVE CONVERSATION TO IGNITE RELATIONSHIP

 SUITED FOR SUCCESS: VOLUME 2

 THE FORMULA CHART FOR LIFE

 THE IMPACT OF INFLUENCE: VOLUME 1

 THE IMPACT OF INFLUENCE: VOLUME 2

 R.O.C.K. SOLID

 STAY ON THE RIGHT P.A.T.H.

 THE IMPACT OF INFLUENCE: VOLUME 3

 BLACK MEN LOVE

 THE IMPACT OF INFLUENCE: VOLUME 4

 THE WINNING MINDSET

 THE IMPACT OF INFLUENCE: VOLUME 5

 CONCRETE CONNECTIONS

To order your autographed copies visit
http://chip-baker-the-success-chronicles.square.site/

www.ingramcontent.com/pod-product-compliance
Lightning Source LLC
Chambersburg PA
CBHW071353080526
44587CB00017B/3083